Writers of Wales

Gwenlyn Parry

Writers of Wales

Gwenlyn Parry

Roger Owen

University of Wales Press

Cardiff 2013

www.uwp.co.uk

British Library Cataloguing-in-Publication Data
A catalogue record for this book is available from the British Library.

ISBN 978-0-7083-2662-6
e-ISBN 978-0-7083-2663-3

The publisher acknowledges the financial support of the Welsh Books Council.

Typeset in Wales by Eira Fenn Gaunt, Fenn Typesetting, Cardiff
Printed by CPI Antony Rowe, Chippenham, Wiltshire

To Sally, with all my love

Contents

Acknowledgements

I am indebted to several members of Gwenlyn Parry's family for their help and kind co-operation while researching this book, for their generosity in showing photographs from their own collections and for providing permission for their reproduction here. I am particularly grateful to Joye Evans Parry and Ann Beynon in this respect: without their support and assistance, many aspects of the work would have been impossible. I also received valuable help from Sian Elin Parry and Llynwen Griffith.

A number of Gwenlyn's close colleagues played an important role in forming my overview of his work and character, and it is my great pleasure to thank them for their perceptive comments and for the great value that they placed on their memories of Gwenlyn: particularly Meredydd Evans, Sion Eirian, Meic Povey, John Ogwen and Maureen Rhys. I am also grateful to Lyn T. Jones, T. James Jones and Endaf Emlyn for their willingness to contribute. During the latter stages of correcting and proofreading the drafts of this book, John Hefin, one of Gwenlyn's closest colleagues and friends over many years, passed away. His contribution to this account of Gwenlyn's life, through his many collaborations with Gwenlyn, through his editorship of the irreverent *Grand Slam: Behind the Scenes of the Classic Film*, his beautifully observed tribute television documentary, *Cofio Gwenlyn*, and his deeply insightful interviews, was invaluable. He was, in addition, a wonderfully warm and generous human being. One had to do very little more than talk to John to understand the kind of respect and deep affection that Gwenlyn inspired in his long-term colleagues, and the thoroughgoing passion for life which underpinned their professional collaboration. I am also very grateful to John's wife and my Aberystwyth colleague, Elin Hefin, for her keen and witty observations on John and Gwenlyn's working relationship.

I was greatly aided by the advice, encouragement and patience of the staff at the University of Wales Press, including Professor M. Wynn Thomas for his comments on the draft, to Sarah Lewis, Siân Chapman and particularly to Dr Angharad Watkins. I also very gratefully acknowledge the assistance of staff at the National Library of Wales in Aberystwyth and at the Gwynedd Archive Service in Caernarfon, particularly Annwen Jones.

I am also indebted to my colleagues and to former colleagues at the Department of Theatre, Film and Television Studies, especially to Professors Hazel Walford Davies and Elan Closs Stephens. Publication of this volume was aided by a grant from Aberystwyth University's Sir David Hughes Parry Fund, which I gladly acknowledge.

Finally, I have received a great deal of love and support from my own family, particularly Sally, Eluned and Rhianedd, who have indulged me throughout; and from Eddie Ladd and Andre Stitt, who have made trips to Cardiff unreasonably comfortable.

In order to ensure a consistency of tone I have translated all quotations from interviews conducted in Welsh, and from Welsh critical studies and articles, and accept full responsibility for any errors, skewed emphases or misappropriation of facts. Quotes from Gwenlyn Parry's plays and interviews are also my translations, unless otherwise stated; and I gratefully acknowledge the permission granted by Ann Beynon to include these in the present study.

Illustrations

Introduction

Y Tŵr ['The tower'], Gwenlyn Parry's most highly regarded stage play, shows us a Man and a Woman going through their lives enclosed within the walls of a Tower. The Tower has four floors, which correspond to four phases in life: infancy and childhood, adolescence and youth, middle age, and finally old age and death. We are not privy to the events on the ground floor, but join the action at the point where the characters move up into adolescence and sexual maturity. Thereafter, during the three acts of the play, we watch them live out their relationship on successive floors of the Tower, where they make love, quarrel, reconcile, and try to find solace in each other's company. At the climax of the play, on the very top floor, the Old Man dies, and the Old Woman waits alone for her own end, fascinated and appalled by the brevity of the life which has passed her by.

However, the action does not quite end there. Her husband suddenly arises from his deathbed and is transformed back into a younger version of himself – the Young Man who was seen in Act I. He calls upon his wife to join him on his journey up the final flight of stairs, out through the very roof of the Tower. His resurrection appears to promise a life hereafter, saving the play from its despairing denouement. But there is a further twist. The Old Woman does not respond to his entreaties. She appears not to have heard him directly; his words may have been a mere reiteration of things said in youth, his appearance possibly an apparition or a memory. He disappears. However, at the very last, she is gently cheered by the sound of a train in the distance. The travails of her life conclude in a moment of ambiguous joy.

Y Tŵr is an important Welsh play, one of only a handful which have proved capable of outlasting their own age, and which genuinely merit close dramaturgical analysis and repeated stage production: to the extent that there is an acknowledged tradition of dramatic writing in Welsh, *Y Tŵr* is one of its mainstays. But what is this Tower, this edifice in which Gwenlyn Parry's characters have been incarcerated? Does it have meaning in itself? And why are we invited to watch as this couple's life runs its course, to end in a combination of incredulity, despair and oblique spiritual hope?

It is the contention of this study that an answer to such questions may tell us much about the relationship between the dramatist and his work. Gwenlyn Parry was a key figure in twentieth-century Welsh drama, both in theatre and television. In their day, his stage plays were seen as important, lauded for their crafted dialogue and powerful theatricality; and a number of them can still be counted as highly effective and persuasive works of theatre. Almost single-handedly, he created and popularized a modernist idiom for Welsh drama, and provided a crucial stimulus to the flowering of the new professional theatre of the 1960s and 1970s. He was also a hugely important figure in Welsh television drama during the same period. His multifarious contributions were widely popular and innovative, and he played a vital role in establishing a distinctive voice for BBC drama in Wales. But there was a distinct difference between Parry's voice and persona as a stage dramatist and as a television writer. His original work for television was largely comic in tone, and was – like Gwenlyn himself – notable for its ebullience, its energy and ready wit, rooted in a distinctly working-class and masculine sense of identity. His stage plays, although certainly not devoid of humour, suggest a very different view of life; and *Y Tŵr* in particular suggests one preoccupied with anxieties and repressed fears, alienated from daily reality, and plagued by doubts about the efficacy of communication.

Y Tŵr is also an important work in relation to Parry's own life and career. It constitutes a pivotal moment in both. Written in 1977–8, when he was in his mid-forties, it is widely considered to be the high point of his artistic achievement. He produced two further plays after *Y Tŵr*, but these were significantly different in a number of ways, departing from the kind of formal configuration and timeless contemporaneity which had come to be considered his trademark: neither received the kind of acclamation which greeted his earlier work. This change in style was in some ways prefigured by *Y Tŵr* itself. It is a play that is preoccupied with incarceration and enclosure, and its characters are captives in a tightly-bounded world of their own making, prisoners within their own biography. It cannot fail to suggest that a comparable feeling might have afflicted the dramatist too. Now in middle age, he found himself curiously abandoned. He had left his native *bro* in north Wales and had settled in Cardiff; but his attachment to the square mile of his childhood was intense and lasting, and a part of him could not be reconciled to life elsewhere. However, at the same time, while he hung on grimly to a part of his childhood, his native *bro* abandoned him. Between the mid-1950s when he left and the mid-1970s when he wrote *Y Tŵr*, it changed dramatically, undoing many of the social, industrial and cultural ties which had given his experiences of childhood and youth such power and authority and such a sense of distinction. Part of him yearned for the immediacy of those experiences; but the Tower – which, tellingly, is not entered until adulthood – acts as an impediment to such a yearning. It is a place of alienation, in which life seems to be *happening* to the characters against their deeper will. Their pre-alienated state is denoted by the opening image of the play, presented as a film projection, which shows a pair of children playing happily on a beach, engrossed in the simple joy of being, and blissfully unaware of that which might await them in adulthood. The Tower, then, whatever its significance as a universal symbol of the human condition, is certainly an anxiety, denoting Parry's own fear that he was somehow denying life to himself. It is a sign of conflict between those aspects of his life which had to be sustained by a prolonged act of will – his sense of his public identity, his career, possibly even his marriage – and those things which had been given to him before he knew it – his capacity for fantasy, his language and his feeling for comradeship. In other words, *Y Tŵr* is his mid-life crisis. Parry needed to write the Tower into existence in order to dispense with it, to shift away from 'authorized' ideas about his life and work, and – whatever the artistic consequences – to try to be more independently inclined as a result.

If there is a 'meaning' to Parry's Tower, then, it lies not so much in its various properties as a metaphor but in its presence as a feeling, as a gradually increasing sense of paralysis. It debilitates the lives of those who are held, engrossed, within it, including the characters in the play, and the creative imagination which created them in the first place. Crucially, it also gradually paralyzes its audience too. *Y Tŵr* is not merely a dramatic proposition – it is also a piece of theatre; and the creeping physical debility of ageing as it affects the characters' bodies is intimately related to the audience's experience in the theatre. The play replicates our paralysis, our surrender of physical intervention during the process of spectating, and its meaning is thus inseparable from the act of looking at it. *Y Tŵr* is thus not just about the fate of the couple whose journey we follow, it is about the whole experience of theatre; and this, once again, is an important and distinctive feature of Gwenlyn Parry's work. His plays, far more so than those of most of his contemporaries, make implicit (and eventually explicit) reference to theatre and theatricality as part of their unfolding action. Thus, the Tower, like the theatre, presents those held in its thrall – the characters and the audience – with 'the full, active texture of existence without living it out' (as noted by the sociologist Jean Duvignaud); and allows both parties to be residually aware of how this spectacle is moving and affecting their own 'sleeping bodies'.[1]

When studying Parry's plays, we need to bear their theatrical nature in mind: their full effect, and thus their inherent meaning, is only really available when considering them as *actions*, represented by actors and submitted for the immediate scrutiny of an audience. As such, they tell us a good deal about the way in which he approached his creativity. Drama became his preferred medium of expression, in theatre and on television, because of its dynamism and transience and because of its combination of immediacy with second-order presentation. This allowed him the opportunity to project those aspects of his writing at which he was most adept – rhythmic dialogue, the imagining and staging of compelling situations – and to elide those which were the cause of anxiety – intellectual or philosophical debate, for example. Drama allowed him to create an intimate bond with his audience while retaining a quality of ambiguity and obliqueness, to create absorbing actions which were never absolutely conclusive or finished, and were vitalized by their status as possibilities.

Another key aspect of drama that interested Parry was its public nature. Although in many ways an introspective writer, he was also committed to public expression, to company and *hwyl*. At several points during his lifetime, he ascribed his interest in drama to his immersion during childhood into a society which prized dialogic exchange as a craft, which required of its members a combative self-expression, particularly in relation to wit and humour. Drama was thus a means of encapsulating that kind of speech, and of emphasizing the special characteristics of speech as a (highly dynamic, tendentious and often unreliable) means of describing one's position in the world. As already implied, Gwenlyn was a consummate performer. He was not an actor as such, but he was wont to hold court among his fellows, often alongside his lifelong friend Rhydderch Jones, and could regale his audience with stories for many hours. The (occasionally grand) narrative arc of the funny story, the puncturing effect of the barbed one-liner, the cut and thrust of comradely banter – these were his preferred and practised modes of expression. Drama furnished him with all of these resources, as well as providing a means of working the Welsh language, of rendering it melodic, pungent, percussive, and – perhaps most importantly of all – fresh to the ears of his listeners.

In all of this, there is a crucial relationship to modernism. One of the effects of the historical decline of the Welsh language during the twentieth century, together with the kind of cultural and social life with which it had been traditionally associated in the Welsh-speaking heartlands of *y Fro Gymraeg*, was to make some of modernism's most pervasive features – anxiety, doubt, introspection and an anguished quest for the restoration of an integral self – aspects of a Welsh identity. This is not to say that every Welsh speaker in Wales suddenly became a modernist during the twentieth century, nor that modernism was suddenly the preferred mode for artists and writers in Wales, nor that those things which had stimulated modernism – the development of advanced technological capitalism for one – required a society in cultural and linguistic crisis in order to flourish; but, to those who were concerned about the fragility and contingency of Welsh-language society and culture, modernism suddenly became peculiarly available as a set of ideas and modes of discourse. Another important general feature of modernism was that it was largely individual as opposed to communal, and presented interpersonal communication as a seriously complex, contingent and compromised activity. In this sense, the basic premise of modernism was that the individual's cognitive and sensory faculties, far from easily or smoothly integrating him into a social world, alienated him by means of their fundamental instability and discontinuity. Furthermore, that same sense of alienation was visited on the individual himself: the idea that he could be in possession of a coherent, knowable 'self' was undermined (after Freud) by the assertion that his immediate experience existed at the level of the unconscious as a chaotic, interpenetrating mass of sense. The 'self' was merely the echo, the (false) reformulation of this immediate experience; and it was rendered doubly false when represented and communicated through discursive language. Thus, cognition, representation and communication were all defined as second-order actions, endlessly and hopelessly chasing after sensory, somatic and nervous stimuli which, while they were originative, causal, and thus 'true', were fundamentally incommunicable.

Gwenlyn Parry was both fascinated and deeply troubled by this kind of definition of modernism. He was keenly aware in his own mind and his own sensibility of the alienated nature of individuality, of the lack at the very core of his subjectivity, as the psychoanalyst Jacques Lacan might put it. But he was also a passionate advocate and defender of the Welsh language; and, in that context, the idea of alienation and incommunicability was anathema to him. Drama became his preferred medium of artistic expression because it allowed him to be true to both halves of the contradiction simultaneously. It allowed him to create work which could muse on the helpless and hopeless condition of the individual thrown into an alienated world, but it also allowed him, by virtue of its form, to restore and possibly even reinstate communication and communion between individuals, albeit temporarily. The performance of drama could create a deep sense of unity in an audience, through a joint effort of attentiveness and a collective, analogous exercise of the imagination.

If this appealed to him, it did so because the circumstances of his own life presented him with a powerful sense of contradiction or conflict between individuated and communal views of being. He was keenly aware of distinctions between himself and the people around him, particularly in terms of class; and his experience of growing up was tainted by a sense of his social inferiority, revealed to him particularly vividly during his school career. But there was another, far more intimate arena for conflicting experiences of personal and communal identity in his life: the family. Parry's familial relationships were intense, his relationship with his mother particularly so. It seems that she was the one who impressed upon her son a moral foundation and a set of expectations for living; in the process, she seems also to have provided him with a vivid sense of constraint, which he internalized as a description of himself and his own state. This same sense of constraint – as we have already seen in relation to *Y Tŵr* – later found external form and expression in aspects of his plays, which, to use Freudian parlance, are consistently concerned with the superego, either in its attempt to control and demonize the free, capricious and libidinous energies of the id, or in the dissipation of those social and external agencies which were formerly responsible for enforcing such controls. Alongside this major conflict between superego and id, the contrast between individuated and communal identity was also a significant feature of Parry's complex relationship with his father; one which was marked by a perception of imbalance between work and home life, between the abundant male-dominated and distinctly dangerous world of the Dinorwic slate quarry and the more private female-dominated hearth, where he seemed to willingly subordinate himself to his wife's rule. It was also marked by his father's absence for six years during the Second World War, during Parry's transition from childhood to adolescence, and by the change which he witnessed in his father's character upon his return. It accounts for many images in Parry's plays of the father figure as a kindly, residually authoritative but fundamentally weak (or weakened) man.

Parry grew into complex and compelling adult life as one with a considerable appetite for living, a great talent and compulsion for storytelling, and a propensity for deep, committed friendships. But he also grew into a acutely phobic individual, suffering from fears and anxieties of all sorts; one who was almost wilful in his lack of organization in many aspects of daily life; and, particularly in relation to the consumption of alcohol, one who was committed to pleasure – although *hwyl* might be a better word – to the point of self-destruction. He was by no means at peace with himself, and was dedicated to artistic creation as a means of temporarily and obliquely attending to the unruliness of his condition.

Gwenlyn Parry's plays have been discussed and analyzed a good deal over the years – mainly, of course, in Welsh. Even though most of his plays have been translated and produced in English at various times, none of these translations has been published; and awareness of his achievement as a writer in English is largely restricted to his writing credits for films such as *Grand Slam* and *A Penny for your Dreams/I Fro Breuddwydion*, as well as *Un Nos Ola Leuad*. In that respect, it is worth noting that this study will pay particular attention to his plays for the theatre as opposed to his work for television and film. This is problematic, as his drama and comedy for television constitute a good deal of his life's work; and they are also significant for having offered him a way of writing which was free from the kind of self-imposed pressures that are evident in his theatre plays. However, his media work, although of considerable importance, is generally difficult to relate directly to his own way of looking at the world because of the fact that much of it was created as a response to ideas and briefs which were not necessarily of his own making in the first instance, and may have been reshaped and modified significantly during production and post-production. Another salient point is that much of his television and film work was collaborative. This complicates any attempt to interpret the work as belonging to or specifically reflecting Gwenlyn's own vision; it is, however, significant in its own right, and deserves to be acknowledged as such. The way in which Parry worked alongside a colleague such as Rhydderch Jones, either as a writer or script editor, and alongside a producer such as John Hefin, with each influencing the other in different ways and to different degrees, could merit a study all of its own. The present study will make reference to some of the more important examples of his television work, but, as part of a series dedicated to the vision of individual writers, it can only really refer to them as accompaniments to his solo work for the theatre stage.

Where his work has been critically discussed, it has been dealt with from a literary and theatrical perspective, but a good deal of the discussion has also been focussed on philosophical, and particularly theological, issues. The most obvious, and exceptional, example is the late Dewi Z. Phillips's authoritative extended study *Dramâu Gwenlyn Parry*. His study considers the stage plays as metaphysical statements about the wider human condition, and interprets them as evidence of a decline in religious faith and of a failure of religious language. In that respect, in spite of its brilliance as a study and its influence on discussions of Parry's plays, it is occasionally concerned with what the plays fail to say rather than what they actually contain. Nonetheless, part of Parry's reputation as a playwright has been based on the view that he managed to elevate Welsh drama to the level of such philosophical discourse without undermining the vitality of the characters' speech and without compromising its popular appeal through 'needless' complexity. In this introductory study of Parry's work, I have no desire to counter Phillips's assertions: however, in general, I will try to avoid the notion that the plays can, or ought to, be read as 'metaphysical' visions of a universal human condition; I will also tend not to treat them as constituting a Welsh approach to Absurdism. Rather, their philosophical aspect will be treated as an outcome of

Parry's writing rather than a motivation for it. He was, after all, an intuitive dramatist, one who allowed the process of writing to take its own course, and to incite or excite its own themes and its own images in the process. He belonged to no particular school or movement, but wrote from the midst of his own personal conflicts, and was true to them, and to the way in which theatre could address their different aspects simultaneously.

In addressing his life and work, then, it is appropriate to take a psychoanalytical perspective from time to time in order to identify and highlight certain 'pressure points', moments in which his suppositions about his own life appear to intervene in his artistic vision and suggest a far more personal concern than may be evident on the surface.

'Llanbabo it is to us and Llanbabo it will remain': Early Life

William Gwenlyn Parry was born in the village of Deiniolen (or Llanbabo), Caernarfonshire on 8 June 1932. His father, William John Parry, was a quarryman at the nearby Dinorwic slate quarry; his mother Katie Parry (née Griffiths) worked for a number of years as a nurse at Eryri hospital in Caernarfon. He was the elder of two children; his sister, Margaret, was five years his junior.

Parry's early recollections portray life in the village as a kind of idyll: '[w]hat a place for a lad to be brought up', he said, 'everything there – mountains [. . .] rivers [. . .] trees [. . .] plenty of room to play tricks'.[1] It was a place in which to dawdle in fields, by streams and in the streets; to play football, and have games of snooker in the local library; to attend plays every week at the vestry of Ebeneser chapel; to pay occasional visits to the makeshift cinema, where films were projected onto canvas; to follow the local silver band; and to spend time among the quarry lads, enjoying their combative wit and acuity. And it was a little world of its own, nestling in a hollow beneath three mountains – Elidir, Moel Riwen and the Bigil. According to one of his favourite allusions, these formed a kind of protective bowl or shell around the inhabitants,[2] one which enclosed the community and helped to define its distinctive identity and vibrant self-sufficiency.

The substance of childhood life in Deiniolen was *hwyl*. Not just a word for 'fun' or 'enjoyment', *hwyl* was hugely important, and deep. For Parry, it was indicative of a whole sense of belonging, of experiencing his own culture's ability to sustain itself through play. It was a means by which he could elevate the ordinary events and circumstances of his life to the level of epic fantasy. Long before he embarked on his career as a writer of drama, *hwyl* was one of the cornerstones of his life. When recounting his travels around the country as a supporter of the famous Deiniolen Silver Band, for example, Parry – although not particularly musical himself – allowed his imagination to run free:

> I'll never forget going with the band to compete in places as far away as Belleview . . . sometimes winning the first prize in our category. And coming back to Deiniolen late at night, in the bus, with the top of the bus opened . . . And we'd come back to Deiniolen and hold the cup aloft, and everyone would be gathered round the Library, shouting 'Hooray!' and receiving us as if we were heroes.[3]

The same *hwyl* was there in his interest in theatre during childhood, although this was hardly exceptional or vocation-defining at this stage. He delighted in the weekly plays staged at Ebeneser (usually by locals, but with occasional visits by companies from the 'the other side of the world' – the south Wales valleys)[4] which consisted mainly of the classics of *y mudiad drama*, the Welsh amateur movement. They were spirited and impassioned but largely unsophisticated productions, as were Parry's own early efforts:

> At the bottom of the village there was a row of empty houses called Cae Tai. In one of these houses, we built a stage out of rocks and old mattresses with flour sacks hanging on a rope as curtains. The entry charge was two soft sweets or one hard sweet such as mint imperials because they lasted longer as you sucked them. They were pretty rudimentary plays, mind you, full of action – such as one throwing a bucket of water over the other, but we had a barrowload of *hwyl*.[5]

Language was crucially important in all of this. Much of the fun that was to be had in and around the quarrying village was generated by the vitality and variety – indeed, the sheer amount – of the vernacular Welsh which issued from the lips of ordinary workers and their families. It provided Parry with a sense of the richness, the native invention and the persuasiveness of everyday speech. It also proved to him how a language could be moulded by the experiences of a specific community in order to create a cohesive and intense sense of local identity which was fundamentally generous in spirit but veritably tribal in its clear demarcation of borders and limits. The very act of naming his home village demonstrated how the vernacular tongue could identify and delineate social strata, distinguishing between insiders and outsiders. Gwenlyn delighted in the fact that he lived in a place which had one name – Deiniolen – 'on the lips of the surrounding gentry', but another 'on the tongues of those of us lads who live there'.[6] For them, and him, it was *Llanbabo* or *Llanbabs*. The dynamism of language, and the way in which it could assume its own kind of authority in the naming of places, in the creation of stories and in combative and communicative exchange between ordinary people, in sheer *hwyl*, was a part of the fabric of his being from the first.

But life in Deiniolen was not all fun and games. Living 'under that old quarry', as Gwenlyn put it in an interview, the Parrys were in a precarious position.[7] The family's economic well-being was under constant threat because of the quarrying industry's peculiar pay structure (there was no guarantee of a regular fixed wage) and because of the physical dangers inherent in the work. Deaths or serious injury in the quarry were not uncommon, and the early sounding of the quarry hooter and the spectacle of the men trailing down the 'incline' from Dinorwic after an accident haunted Parry from an early age. Such things always seemed to happen, he said, when they were least expected, 'when everyone was feeling happy . . . it was always sunny when something unpleasant happened'.[8] In spite of such fears, Parry identified very strongly with the working-class society of industrial Caernarfonshire: indeed, his first stated ambition was to be a quarryman like his father. This was not so much for the work, of course, as for the grit and implicit sense of heroism with which a quarryman's life seemed to be imbued. Parry admired the rugged honesty of a life spent toiling in the company of male fellows, in which a deep mutual understanding and comradeship was implicit; and although he was never to be a quarryman himself, he made sure that those values were a prominent part of his own working life.

Parry began his educational career at the local Gwaun Gynfi primary school. It was not, at first, a happy time. Schooling gave him his first experience of systematic injustice and social prejudice, and – with a few highly honourable exceptions – it left an over-whelmingly negative impression on him. For a number of years, he was not identified as a particularly bright pupil, and was all but ignored by a headmaster whose contempt for those from the lower social class was marked, and who regarded the son of a quarryman living on the council estate at Hafod Olau as hardly worth educating at all. Fortunately, things changed when a new headmaster, Richard Jones BSc, took over as headmaster of Gwaun Gynfi towards the end of Gwenlyn's time there. Jones applied a methodical scientific approach to the testing and analysis of his pupils, and recognized a precociousness in Gwenlyn, who was at that point languishing in twenty-fourth place out of a class of thirty. He challenged and encouraged him enough to help him secure a scholarship to Brynrefail Grammar School; and Parry suggested that his later interest in science may have been rooted in his desire to emulate his mentor.

He was seven years old when the war was declared. His father, being in a reserved occupation, was not required to join up; but, spurred on by a sense of duty, he did so out of choice and became a field cook in the 8th Army (Parry did joke occasionally that his father had gone off to war in order to get away from his mother's domineering presence at home). As he left, in an almost consciously Freudian gesture, William John gave Gwenlyn the key to his snooker cue locker, telling him to look after it – along with his wife and daughter – until he returned. From then until the end of the conflict, there was little if any contact between the family and the father. Relationships within the Parry household began to change. His mother, who had previously spent a good deal of time looking after her children, went out to work in a munitions factory in nearby Llanberis, a move which had the effect of suddenly giving her an almost proverbially masculine identity in Gwenlyn's mind: 'that's when I had one of the most shattering experience of my life,' he joked, years later. 'Seeing my mother coming back to the house one night after work wearing long trousers ... And she wore them in the house for ever after this time.'[9] But his own masculine identity began to grow during his father's absence, and gradually, obliquely, he assumed the status of the (little) man of the house. Towards the end of her life, Margaret Parry fondly recalled the sense of protection which she derived from his presence as an older brother: 'he was the one who kept us going ... on nights when he heard that the planes were going to fly over us ... he'd say "Let's all sleep together tonight", and so the three of us would go to sleep in the big bed, ... with Gwenlyn in the middle looking after his mother and his little sister.'[10]

Even as he matured into his role, however, his father returned, a conquering hero, and discharged Gwenlyn from such protective responsibilities. Aged thirteen, he was asked to relinquish the key to the snooker cue locker. Having lost a father, gained a masculinized mother, and been promoted to a kind of manhood himself during the worst of the war, Gwenlyn was now returned to juvenility. But he also gained a 'brother' of sorts. William John was a changed man:

> He looked older than I had thought, and different from what I remembered. He was quieter if anything, and he would discuss things with me – even ask my opinion on some things. I was no longer his little boy, but his big boy ... So the estrangement that had occurred between my father and me had created a different relationship; I would almost say that it was now the relationship of two brothers. And so it remained throughout his life.[11]

The war had, unexpectedly, brought about a positive development in their relationship; however, the duality implicit in Gwenlyn's impression of his father was not easy to accommodate or resolve. Enhanced admiration, although genuine, was only one aspect of his response to this experience. The unsettling effect of the disruption of the family, the constant dread of the War Office telegram, and the change in the sense of order after the war, seems to have undermined Parry's sense of the stability of the social world, and emphasized its contingency. While he associated his mother with a sense of

security ('Mam was the symbol of being "in control", . . . it was
mam who was at home – looking after us . . . There was no fear
while mam was in the question'),[12] Parry noted how he associated
his father with danger, and thus with theatre:

> my father was the symbol of danger for me – it was my father who
> worked in the quarry, it was my father who went away to the Army
> . . . that's why I tend to talk about my father, because my father was
> associated with the dangerous thing. And that is perhaps what is
> theatrical – the dangerous thing.[13]

His father, whose silence in the face of Katie's authority around
the house may have previously suggested a certain emasculation,
was given a greater authority by his experiences, and was now a
figure whom Parry could openly admire: 'He taught me that one
of the greatest sins that exists is to hurt someone deliberately, be
it with a word or a fist. He also taught me to stick by the truth and
to give my opinion plainly without fear or favour even if that
should cost me in terms of status or money.'[14]

Parry's years at Brynrefail Grammar School largely constituted
a return to the bad times at Gwaun Gynfi. Once again, he found
himself routinely overlooked. According to Parry, the headmaster
at Brynrefail had 'not an ounce of interest' in the Welsh language
and culture, a fact which was indicated by the choice of school song,
'Forty Years On', which it shared with Harrow (among others).[15]
Again, there were those who provided inspiration, including several
science teachers, as well as Miss Cadi Evans, who excited Parry's
interest in Welsh literature; but he was forcibly informed that the
pursuit of arts subjects was no route to employment for a man. But
there was no redeeming Richard Jones-like figure here, and the
experience of exclusion through a combination of class prejudice
and anglicization led to a lifelong sensitivity and rage against
overbearing authority and injustice.

But Richard Jones himself was not finished with Gwenlyn. A few
years after they met at Gwaun Gynfi, he was nurturing Parry as a
Wesleyan lay preacher, a practice which constituted an alternative,

and far less prejudicial, kind of education. Parry, of course, had been a chapelgoer throughout his life, but his educational 'salvation' by Richard Jones made religion mean a good deal more to him than it might have done otherwise. Though he was a regular attender at Tabernacl chapel and Sunday school – he was encouraged, if not required, to do so three times every Sunday by his mother – religion was less a matter of Christian faith to him than of succour through ritual and stimulation through performance. He was captivated by the sense of theatre he found in chapel life: 'Hearing Twm Nefyn or Tegla Davies [preaching] was basically nothing to do with my soul – or my sin – it was to do with great entertainment.'[16] His own practice as a lay preacher was based on the simple division of elements in life into good and evil, a 'habit' which brought him 'a lot of comfort', and had a distinct influence on his approach to the practice of writing for theatre later in life:

> I'm sure I composed dozens of sermons – with the help of Richard Jones, and . . . the shape of a sermon or the outline of a sermon is very similar to a play – to start with you have three headings in a sermon and three acts in a play, and a sermon develops to a kind of twist in the tail, just as a three act play has some kind of kick in the tail and a kind of moral . . . And there are some who have said that my weakness as a dramatist is that I try to include some kind of moral at the end. Well, that could be Richard Jones's fault for making me a lay preacher.[17]

The onset of adulthood brought with it a dual crisis. Towards the end of his school career, the sudden death of a friend dealt him a blow which made him ask some fundamental questions. Why had God allowed such a thing to happen? Why, indeed, did He allow war, and human suffering? Aware that such questions about the Almighty's intervention in the world were something of a cliché, he was nonetheless troubled by them, and unable to form satisfactory answers. His faith began to weaken: 'I remember looking out of the window one day at a tree . . . in the garden, and coming to the conclusion that God doesn't exist . . . That it was all rubbish.'[18] At about the same time, after completing his education at Brynrefail in 1950 (having taken his Higher Grade exams in physics, chemistry and mathematics), he was called up for National Service. His first instinct was to refuse the call-up on the basis of conscience. However, the thought of acting upon his beliefs intimidated him deeply. He knew the kind of ostracization which awaited those who refused to enlist, having himself been among the village lads who revelled in hurling abuse at conscientious objectors during the war. He now had to decide where his own true sympathies lay.

In the midst of these crises, something in his bond with the native 'shell' of childhood experience was broken. Having been formed by so much of what he had seen and experienced within it, he now found himself outside, alienated both in terms of his religious belief and the exercise of his conscience. It was a particularly difficult moment in relation to the example set for him by his father: he was a Wesleyan deacon, and though of a gentle disposition, had gone to the war and had returned a hero, along with all those others from the village who had been 'accepted back with honour, and received medals'. How could Gwenlyn dishonour all that?: 'How could I be a "conchi" in Deiniolen?', he asked.[19] Of course, his father had been changed by the war, and it had been his stories and reports of the horrors of war that had suggested to Gwenlyn that the only honourable course under the circumstances would be to stand up for the right, and refuse enlistment. One of these two 'fathers' was sure to be disappointed in him.

Ultimately, he tried to compromise, and ended up disappointing himself: he accepted his conscription, but enlisted in a non-combat role as a nurse in the RAF. While this tactic removed the impasse, it was evidently not enough to dispel a sense of failure. Later in life, when discussing the events of his youth, he pointedly repeated the charge of cowardice against himself: 'I should certainly have been a conscientious objector at that time but I was too much of a *cachwr*'; and he added that, though he had tried to stick to his father's example throughout his life, 'I failed when I got the "call-up" to go to the armed forces.'[20]

However, his genuine moral scruples notwithstanding, Parry spent a largely happy time as an RAF nursing orderly. Posted at RAF Valley on Anglesey, he took to the work, and it in turn provided him with important thematic material and medical detail for some of his later plays as well as qualifications and skills (such as embalming) which, he would joke, set him apart from other writers.[21] It was also an opportunity to meet a great many different individuals, to hear about their problems and understand something of their lives at particularly difficult moments. Once again, this was a rich source of material: 'People in pain are keen to confess much to someone', he noted later.[22] This curiously and unexpectedly Chekhovian entrée into a new world and a wider society left him, in his own estimation, 'a more mature man – more patient and less selfish'[23] – a distinct echo of his description of his father following his return from armed service.

Upon discharge from the RAF, he resumed his education. He had hoped to study Welsh at the university in Bangor, but was not considered for entry because his background had been in the sciences; and so he enrolled at the nearby Bangor Normal College – a training college for teachers which, although not academically on a par with the university, allowed him to pursue Welsh literature as well as mathematics and science. There, in addition to his formal studies, he was able to pursue further interests in drama, a subject which was much in vogue at the teacher training colleges around Wales at the time and an area in which creative opportunities abounded for those not weighed down by the demands of an Honours degree. Parry soon began to cut his teeth in theatre work by assisting in college productions with directing, stage management and, occasionally, acting. He tried almost everything, in fact, except writing.

After graduating from the Normal, he left Wales and took a job teaching mathematics and science at Holloway Road Boys' School in King's Cross, London. He jokingly suggested, years later, that his reasons for leaving Wales were not related to his career prospects but rather to the opportunity of being able to see some of the best theatre of the day.[24] Be that as it may, it was a move which mirrored that of a number of other important Welsh-language dramatists, such as John Gwilym Jones, who also spent some time in London in the 1930s and was influenced by the West End theatre; Saunders

Lewis, who was deeply influenced by theatre outside Wales, and whose play *Blodeuwedd* was directly inspired by his experience of seeing Sybil Thorndike as Medea on the London stage; and W. S. Jones ['Wil Sam'], whose highly idiosyncratic dramatic writing owed much of its vitality to his longstanding interest in Irish drama and frequent visits to the theatres of Dublin. For all their concern for the Welsh language and theatre, and alongside their nationalist beliefs, these most influential Welsh playwrights of the twentieth century – Gwenlyn Parry among them – required the regular experience of metropolitan, and particularly London, stages in order to hone their theatrical craft.

Together with his visits to the West End, Parry continued to be involved in theatre production on a smaller scale with the distinctly ambitious drama society of the London Welsh Club. The club provided him with a kind of 'home from home' and an anchor for his social life in London; as did the many London chapels, which were an important meeting point for Welsh expatriates. And it was in one of these, Tabernacl at King's Cross, that Parry met Joye Davies. Joye was also working as a teacher, at a local primary school, and the relationship between her and Gwenlyn soon became a permanent one. Their life in London was not particularly comfortable, and, although both managed to eke out a living for themselves on their meagre salaries, access to luxuries – such as visits to the theatre and the opera – was limited to about once a month. Her view of Gwenlyn at this time was of a young man with considerable creative talent, but with no real interest in playwriting as such – indeed, in looking back at that period, it was quite surprising to think that he was destined to be a writer for the theatre. He wrote poetry (winning the London Welsh Eisteddfod Chair three times) and painted; but he still had not taken to drama as an outlet.

They married in Caersalem, Pontyberem in April 1958, and returned to London; but both soon received offers of work back in Wales, Gwenlyn at Dyffryn Ogwen School in Bethesda, Joye in Swansea: since Gwenlyn had received his offer first, it was decided that they should return to north Wales. They first moved back to Deiniolen, but then, after Joye found employment at Maesincla school, they set up home in Caernarfon, where they lived for the next ten years.

'Why leave London?', he asked rhetorically in a radio broadcast in 1989. Why leave behind the London Welsh Club, the West End? His answer is instructive:

Because there was some gnawing in the pit of one's stomach which said, 'This is not where you should be, you know'. Something always draws me back. 'A chick born in hell wants to stay in hell', or as [a] hero of mine put it: 'God help me, I cannot escape from this.'[25]

It is worth pausing momentarily to consider the way in which Gwenlyn phrases this recollection. It is not unexpected per se to hear him state his desire to return to Wales through the conventional nostalgic-romantic language of *hiraeth*, and through literary quotation. Nonetheless, the sheer obliqueness with which he expresses himself is revealing: in describing this major decision in his life, he switches from the impersonal to the personal voice and back again, and refers to himself in the first, second and third person: he is 'one', he is 'you', he is 'me', 'a chick', and, through the filter of quotation, 'I'. Whatever this might indicate, it does not project an integrated sense of personal conviction. His desire to return somehow just 'happens' to him, rather than being directly motivated and claimed as a matter of his own volition. And, moreover, such shifts are not untypical of other remarks about his own life and career, particularly those made in interview or in radio broadcasts: the disconnectedness in his reference to himself is consistent. Obviously, we must remain slightly circumspect about all of this; these particular remarks were made in 1989, thirty years after the events they purport to describe, and they may have more to do with his state of mind at the end of the 1980s than at the end of the 1950s. But they are intriguing, and none more so than his allusion to the final line of *Hon*, T. H. Parry-Williams's famous poem. Parry's vacillating self-expression is entirely consistent with Parry-Williams's failing resolve to deny his own innate, 'gnawing' voice. Like his literary hero, Parry claims to be driven back home by a force beyond his conscious control, one which – against his better judgement, and against his will – reveals to him a potently integrated self, from which he cannot escape, God help him.

By 1989, of course, he had escaped; and 'she – '*hon*', the Wales of his childhood – had escaped him too. The idea that the place in which he had been born and reared, in which he had experienced some of the defining crises of his young life, the idea that this place still had knowledge of him, and still *contained* him, was a fantasy. But by then, he had spent the best part of his career animating and sustaining that fantasy through his dramatic writing.

2

'God help me, I cannot escape from this': *Three Short Plays*

Having settled in Caernarfon in 1959, the Parrys took an active part in the local cultural life. It was around this time that Gwenlyn began to write drama in earnest; but he pursued this interest alongside more general theatre work too. With John Gwilym Jones, former BBC producer and lecturer in Welsh at Bangor, he had helped to establish Theatr Fach Eryri, a small but ambitious company run at Glynllifon, where he continued to direct, and occasionally perform on stage himself. Gwenlyn and Joye also found themselves a niche as part of a group of artists, writers and other interested parties who would meet on a Tuesday night at the Newborough Arms in Palace Street. The pub was an important hub, whose landlord Harris Thomas and his wife Stella had decided to try to promote the work of local artists by granting spaces to them to show and discuss their work, to the happy accompaniment of the Newborough's ale. This 'upstairs' clientele included such notable painters as Selwyn Jones and Victor Neep; 'downstairs', meanwhile, the Newborough would occasionally be host to extraordinarily colourful local characters such as 'Wil Napoleon, Mons and the gang'.[1] Both of these groups delighted Parry, albeit in very different ways: he had a marked interest in visual art and frequently produced his own sketches and paintings; but he also loved the mischievous exploits and near-legendary storytelling of the lads in *y dre* ['the town']. The coexistence of the two worlds was one of those features of town life which made Gwenlyn feel particularly at home there. As he put it himself, 'Llanbabs made me what I am, but Caernarfon . . . put the blade on my sword.'[2]

He now produced his first play, *Y Ddraenen Fach*, and was encouraged by his friend and fellow member of the Newborough coterie, the dramatist and teacher Huw Lloyd Edwards, to submit it for the original short play competition at the Dyffryn Maelor National Eisteddfod in 1961, where Parry shared the first prize. The adjudicator at the Dyffryn Maelor National Eisteddfod, Eic Davies, praised the play for its compactness and for its suitability for staging – an important consideration in a competition dedicated to the creation of entertaining and producible drama for local audiences.

Y Ddraenen Fach ['The little hawthorn'] (1961)[3]

It is set in the cellar of a bombed-out house 'somewhere on the coast of North Africa', on Christmas Eve, 1942. Four Allied soldiers are trapped inside, the hawkish middle-aged Green and young Martin, and the more conciliatory middle-aged Lewis and young Williams. Initially, they discuss the possibility of escaping, but, as the action settles down, their dialogue turns to family matters, and to Lewis's photograph of his wife and children outside their mountainside cottage – 'Y Ddraenen Fach'. Lewis recounts his father's lesson about the thorn bush, which exposes its barbs in winter, but is covered in flower come the spring: 'mean and prickly today but flower-laden and beautiful tomorrow. Goodness comes from the vilest things – occasionally.'[4]

Williams – a failed conscientious objector – prompts an argument about the specific difference between cold-blooded murder and killing in the line of duty, and, amid memories of Christmases spent at home, recalls the story of the Christmas truce during the First World War. This leads to a plan to approach the German besiegers with Christmas greetings. As the soldiers prepare to draw lots to decide which of them will make the approach, they are disturbed by a noise from above; whereupon a young German soldier climbs down to the cellar carrying a white cloth. He bids them a merry Christmas in his own language, but, while reaching for a note inviting them to celebrate Christmas with his equally beleaguered colleagues, he is unceremoniously shot by Martin.

Y Ddraenen Fach is not a particularly auspicious debut. Indeed, it is about as dry and dutifully moralistic as a work by someone of Gwenlyn's undoubted imagination and energy could be. However, it does exemplify three key factors in his work which remained in place throughout his career: his decision to write autobiographically, or at least from close personal experience; his tendency to imitate some of his contemporaries; and finally – thankfully – the power of his underlying sense of theatre.

There are several elements in *Y Ddraenen Fach* which relate closely to Parry's own experience. Its title – which in the play is the name of Lewis's home – was taken from Joye's grandparents' home on Llangyndeyrn Mountain, the ruins of which she and Gwenlyn visited together. More importantly, it drew upon, and paid tribute to, aspects of his father's war experience in North Africa; and it also referred directly to the crisis of conscience which had affected Gwenlyn at the time of his call-up for National Service. One of the central exchanges in the play, between the young Williams and his older colleague Lewis, is clearly a kind of dialogue between Gwenlyn and his father, with the older man gently but firmly defusing Williams's more individualistic argument for pacifism: 'I have a wife and children at home', he tells him; 'Do you think that I would be able to watch someone else coming over here to fight for them? Even if you're not prepared to defend your country, you have to defend your family.'[5]

In terms of its dramatic rhetoric, *Y Ddraenen Fach* is desperately unsubtle, and clearly influenced by the kind of amateur theatre which Parry had observed during his youth, as witnessed by Eic Davies's comments at the National Eisteddfod. It is also undoubtedly a take on Willis Hall's Malayan War drama, *The Long and the Short and the Tall*, which Parry had seen towards the end of his time in London. That, too, is a play which concerns the conflict between a group of soldiers who have found themselves detached and hemmed in behind enemy lines. However, whereas Hall succeeds in asking serious moral questions about the culpability of British soldiers in the mistreatment of a Japanese prisoner of war, Parry manages only a cloying homeliness in his attempt to suggest a common humanity among the soldiers on both sides. He tries to achieve the same moral and dramatic intensity as Hall in only a fraction of the time, and the credibility of his play suffers because of the restricted development of the action. The soldiers' incarceration in the cellar is a situation rich in possibilities, but is sadly unrealized by their discussion of ethics and family memories, and their negotiation of a plan to contact their German besiegers. Parry's lack of conviction in this moralistic approach to writing is also revealed by the fact that the play's melodramatic conclusion abruptly – and conveniently – curtails the action at the point where the audience's sense of moral speculation might truly be tested. We are left wondering what could really happen if these soldiers did abandon their conflict to go to play football with each other. There are far more dramatic possibilities implicit in continuing the action through to the point of ceasefire and collaboration than in any pity we may feel for the death of the German soldier.

But beyond the trite subject matter, there are elements in *Y Ddraenen Fach* which hint at a more sophisticated theatrical craft. Though it produces some rather clunking dialogue, Parry's love for the vitality of spoken Welsh is evident. He experiments here with north and south Walian accents, a fact which reflects his new-found familiarity with the rhythms of semi-industrial Carmarthenshire following his marriage to Joye. The simplicity of the play's staging is also theatrically effective. It creates a considerable feeling of claustrophobia, and a sense of anxiety about what lies beyond the visible confines of the stage; it also places the character drama in a starkly featureless context. All of these devices would figure prominently in Parry's later plays, and their presence even in this comparatively undistinguished early piece suggests that Parry's instincts as a dramatist were in truth more inclined towards the dramatic vision of contemporaries such as Beckett and Pinter than to a comparatively realistic playwright like Willis Hall.

For all its faults, *Y Ddraenen Fach* won another National Eisteddfod prize in 1962, in the short play performance competition when performed by the London Welsh Club drama society. This group was, of course, very well known to Gwenlyn, and included a number of his old London acquaintances along with two colleagues whom he had befriended after leaving the city: Rhydderch Jones, who played the young Williams, and Ryan Davies. These two were to play a hugely important part in Gwenlyn's creative life. He had known Rhydderch for a number of years, but the two had become firm friends, along with Ryan, in 1959 at the National Eisteddfod in Caernarfon, where they had taken leading roles in the London Welsh Club's *noson lawen*.[6] Though he was leaving London, Parry had acted as compère as a kind of farewell gesture. Their act was hugely successful, and marked the beginning of a creative, comic partnership between the three of them that would culminate in the extraordinarily popular BBC sitcom *Fo a Fe*, which ran from 1970 to 1976 and which was only curtailed by Ryan's untimely death in 1977.

Working alongside Ryan and Rhydderch sharpened Parry's already keen appetite for riotous fun, but it also influenced his sense of theatricality. Their *noson lawen* act was notable for its energetic and occasionally inspired use of improvisation, one of Ryan's great gifts as an entertainer; and it proved to Gwenlyn that a performance did not have to be particularly earnest or 'well made' in order to be cumulatively powerful and crafted. Variable dynamics and momentum, along with virtuosic use of language, could carry a performance by themselves, regardless of their disruptive effect on 'clean' definitions of situation and character. The same could be said of Dylan Thomas's *Under Milk Wood*, another play which deeply affected and influenced Gwenlyn at this time. Together, these influences helped to inform and shape Parry's second play, one which was as different from *Y Ddraenen Fach* as one could imagine.

Provisionally entitled *Un, Dau, Tri* ['One, two, three'], it was written in 1962 and entered for the short original play competition at the Llanelli National Eisteddfod. Unlike *Y Ddraenen Fach*, however, it did not prove successful. It was placed only in the second class by the adjudicator, Emyr Humphreys, and was criticized for 'becoming mired in the stereotypical' as well as for being too demanding for production by an ordinary amateur company (indeed, Humphreys feared that it 'might ask too much . . . even of most professional producers').[7] But Gwenlyn persisted with it, and submitted a revised version for the same competition a year later, under a new title, *Poen yn y Bol*. This time, it was awarded joint first prize and praised for its satire by the adjudicator, the prolific populist author and commentator J. Ellis Williams: the play, he said, was 'bound to shock some elements of the audience when performed', but added that this was 'no bad thing sometimes.'[8]

This was a reversal of fortune much to Parry's liking, and was added to his already burgeoning store of humorous tales. In this case, he would announce that he once had a play dumped unceremoniously at the bottom of the fifth class in a National Eisteddfod competition and branded as hopeless, only to have the self-same work declared the winner (without further emendation) a year later; thus happily proving the essential folly and fallibility of critics and adjudicators. As Huw Roberts noted, although this tale contained a kernel of truth, it would have been unlike Gwenlyn to undermine it by resorting to factual accuracy.[9] He was not one to let the truth get in the way of a good story.

Poen yn y Bol ['A pain in the belly'] (1962)

The play is a highly compact account of the life of Bili and Neli Puw (née Huws). It begins with Bili, a middle-aged man, undergoing an appendectomy, and being given an anaesthetic. As he loses consciousness – counting from one to ten, but getting no further than three – the stage shifts into a representation of a school playground. Here, the young Bili and Neli establish an immature affection for each other and the children are generally terrorized by amorphous figures of authority, Jôs Bach Scŵl ['Little Jones the schoolmaster'] and the *Gofalwr* [caretaker]. Time is compressed: Bili and Neli's childish games of kiss-chase are suddenly transformed into a pretext for marriage, and they find themselves criticized and ostracized when it is discovered that Neli is pregnant. They are almost simultaneously expelled from the chapel community and married – in both cases by the *Gofalwr*, who, donning a dog collar, becomes the minister who carries out both procedures (he retains his votive brush throughout). Bili then finds employment as a teacher and Neli gives birth to an injured rabbit, but the pressures of a relatively impoverished family life dull their affection for each other. Bili is reduced to approaching a local councillor for promotion, an indignity which is transformed into a chaotic public auction; he also begins to feel increasingly ill as his appendicitis (caused ostensibly by 'eating green apples' and rushing into marriage) takes hold. The play ends with the sudden and vague outbreak of a war, with Bili accused of cowardice and put on trial as a conscientious objector. He is found guilty, and sentenced to be tortured by the surgeon and nurses from the opening scene of the play: as he collapses in terror, the stage reverts to its original configuration, and the surgeon declares drily that the patient will soon be fully healed.

Where *Y Ddraenen Fach* had used Willis Hall as a model, *Poen yn y Bol* appears to follow a number of different sources. The first, as noted, is *Under Milk Wood*. The episodic nature and extreme mobility of Thomas's play is echoed throughout, as is his practice of reducing character relationships and situations to a single, memorably acerbic, stage gesture. It also has the quality of being a 'play for voices'. Although intended for the stage, its fluidity of form, poetic anti-realism and vocally-driven characterization would make it highly appropriate for schematic theatre production or for radio. Moreover, a number of the prevalent themes and character relationships in the play could be seen as a homage to Thomas. *Poen yn y Bol*'s rhythmic flow and its overt concern with sexuality, for example, owes much to the ripeness of Thomas's vision of village life, as does his use of songs and verses and his selection of characters – impudent schoolchildren, carping neighbours, harridan wives and henpecked husbands.

Poen yn y Bol differs from *Under Milk Wood* in its gradual deterioration from childish innocence into an alienated and ultimately nightmarish adulthood. In that respect, it owes a debt to another important influence, namely Ionesco; and especially to those early plays of his such as *The Lesson* or *Rhinoceros* in which an individual finds himself progressively isolated by (often bizarre) logic, circumstance or the power of authority. Interestingly enough, Ionesco seems to have shared Parry's sense of childhood freshness and innocence undone by the banalities of adult life: after a moment of epiphany in his early teenage years, he famously felt as if he had lost something fundamental and beautiful, and always hankered after the clarity and vividness of that experience in his later life. His 'absurdism' was merely a reflection of the world as it appeared to him following that primal loss. In Parry's plays, too, even as early as *Poen yn y Bol*, there is an abiding concern for the fate of the meek, often childlike, individual in a world of malevolence, corruption and slightly unhinged adult violence.

In that sense, the play cannot fail to remind a contemporary reader of a major Welsh work of the same period, namely Caradog Pritchard's novel *Un Nos Ola Leuad* ['One moonlit night']. Pritchard was another of Gwenlyn's literary heroes, and was working as the night editor of the *Daily Telegraph* while Parry was living in London during the 1950s. The two met, and Pritchard was heartened to find a fellow Arfonian from a quarrying background living in the city. According to Parry, *Un Nos Ola Leuad* existed as a radio play at that time, and Pritchard would occasionally telephone Gwenlyn in the dead of night with questions about local dialect and the specific vocabulary of quarrying men; he even asked Parry to take a role in the play.[10] But the BBC rejected the script, and so it first saw the light of day as a novel, published in 1961. Its publication date makes it something of a close call as a direct influence on *Poen yn y Bol*, but its surrealist parochialism certainly has affinities with Parry's play (as well, of course, as *Under Milk Wood*, which may well have been a direct influence on Pritchard too). Like *Un Nos Ola Leuad*, and unlike most of Gwenlyn's other works, *Poen yn y Bol* allows the process of dramatic presentation to be defined and shaped by the traumatic inertia experienced by the lead character. Bili Puw's passive experience of his life as a spectacle parading itself crazily and uncontrollably before him is more than a little reminiscent of the contorted memories of Pritchard's anonymous narrator: both their visions take on monstrous forms as a result of a deeper, and largely unspoken, malaise which afflicts their lives. *Poen yn y Bol*, then, is neatly balanced between these various literary and theatrical influences. But it is also a work which prefigures some important ideas and devices in Parry's later plays. Like them, and as in *Y Ddraenen Fach*, it makes copious use of Parry's own experiences as dramatic material, comically transforming a school into a nightmarish environment presided over by the hysterically anxious Jôs Bach and the bullying *Gofalwr*. In that sense, it is a gleefully cathartic two-fingered salute to many of Parry's own experiences of school life (moreover, it must also be remembered that Gwenlyn, like Bili Puw, had crossed the classroom floor, and gone from schoolboy to teacher in a relatively short space of time). The two school figures also have much in common with later character-pairings in Gwenlyn's work: Jôs Bach is a fretful, failing authority figure given to fantastical delusions (of a religious kind, in this case), while the *Gofalwr* is a boorish tyrant who induces terror through the wielding of a kind of phallic insignia. Both figures are taken up in various ways in later plays such as *Tŷ ar y Tywod* and *Y Ffin*.

Poen yn y Bol's references to religion are particularly interesting in the way that they prefigure later plays. From the beginning, there is a constant use of pseudo-Biblical reference. As soon as he succumbs to the anaesthetic, for example, we hear the voice of Bili Puw the patient setting the scene: 'And the Earth was beautiful and full as a barrel, because darkness was on the deep, but [. . .] but Jôs Bach Scŵl said "Let there be light".'[11] Thereafter, the play presents a struggle between the light of education which leads, almost tragically, to the pitfalls of adult life, and the darkness of the unrestrained libidinous energy most truthfully and plausibly identified with the world of childhood: and, of course, the consumption of an apple (followed by several more) leads Bili Puw out of the relative bliss of childhood into the travails of knowledge. Jôs Bach Scŵl is similarly overcome by the cares of adult, married life, and finds himself a 'martyr' to the cause. But, had the censor not stepped in to moderate Gwenlyn's language, Bili's reply to this complaint would have been even more pointed in its religious reference:

> JÔS BACH SCŴL: Bills! Bills! Until the trap crushes everything to pieces, and my hands are full of holes like a sieve.
> NELI AS A CHILD: Like a pepper pot, sir!
> JÔS BACH SCŴL: Like a sieve!
> BILI AS A CHILD: Like Jesus Christ, sir.
> JÔS BACH SCŴL: (*shocked*) What?
> BILI AS A CHILD AND THE CHILDREN: (*reciting, as one*) Like Jesus Christ, sir.
> JÔS BACH SCŴL: (*considering the matter and agreeing*) Yes.[12]

Jôs Bach's bearing is instantly transformed, and he serenely intones a recitation from the Gospels in defence of the schoolchildren against the *Gofalwr*'s offer to 'settle them . . . to beat them black and blue' with his brush.[13] The *Gofalwr*'s distinct lack of mercy is another interesting aspect of *Poen yn y Bol*: he is a protean and rather terrifying character who, from the outset, is bent on dispensing censure and punishment without discrimination. Given the play's initially child-centred perspective, the *Gofalwr* evidently constitutes a grotesque father figure, an 'obscene paternalistic authority',[14] who wields his brush at every opportunity like a phallic insignia, even when transformed into the minister who 'excommunicates' Bili and Neli for conceiving a child out of wedlock. The presence of such an overtly Freudian figure or device is quite surprising here, but it reoccurs frequently in much of Parry's later work (to the point where one sometimes wonders whether Gwenlyn is mischievously prompting or pre-empting a Freudian interpretation). In this case, the *Gofalwr* uses his phallic insignia in order to advocate the sweeping away of those whom he perceives as wrongdoers; and his sermon as minister confirms his obsessively broad concern with cleanliness – not only of the school but of the soul: 'the brush sweeps, friends, sweeps and sweeps until everything shines like the seat of my trousers. That's what He did in the Garden of Eden – sweep! He swept them out to toil on the earth.'[15]

The extent to which *Poen yn y Bol* borrows its poetic flow, its dramaturgy and aspects of its narration from other sources ultimately makes it little more than an exercise in dramatic craft, an apprentice piece. However, its uncompromising imagery and its riotous energy make it a vastly more successful work than *Y Ddraenen Fach*, and – certain historical changes in social attitudes towards marriage and the portrayal of children notwithstanding – it remains a producible drama. Curiously, its potential longevity owes much to that reductive stereotyping which was criticized by Emyr Humphreys on its first submission to the Eisteddfod competition in 1962. Its descent into cliché is, in many ways, wholly self-conscious: it is a portrayal of the individual volition consumed by the forces of social, moral and theatrical convention, the same central device that could be seen – and lauded – in more mature circumstances in *Y Tŵr*. Here, as there, and with a pointed disregard for the main characters' sense of their own identity, time creates biographical roles for them to occupy, and then destroys them, leaving them bewildered and ultimately alienated by its giddying momentum.

Poen yn y Bol was not Parry's only experiment with Ionescoan drama. There was another, far less reputable, adventure into this field in which Gwenlyn played a role: *Y Ffynnon* ['The fountain'], or *La Fontaine*, a cod-absurdist prank presented at the Welsh Students' Collegiate Drama Festival of 1964. It was billed at the festival as a new Welsh translation by Gareth Miles of 'one of the early works of Eugene Ionesco', and presented on stage by a group of students mostly drawn from the university in Bangor. A prank it may have been, but the perpetrators were not without craft and experience. According to legend, they included the students themselves (among them the young Dafydd Glyn Jones, soon to be a charismatic scholar), the dramatists Huw Lloyd Edwards, W. S. Jones and John Gwilym Jones, and Parry himself, all of whom, according to Gareth Miles in 2008, created the play as an exercise in '"automatic writing": that is, everyone in turn throwing a line, a word or an exclamation into the creative pot.'[16]

The play had been motivated by a distinctly juvenile urge to wreak revenge on the *Western Mail* drama critic D. R. Davies, who had disappointed some of the students with his cursory review of their production of John Gwilym Jones's *Hanes Rhyw Gymro*. Some discerning critics, including Jacob Davies and Norah Isaac, were fooled by the play, but D. R. Davies was apparently not, as witness his not-so-subtle description of *Y Ffynnon* as 'a brilliant dramatic reading in Welsh . . . translated by Gareth Miles from UNESCO.'[17] Jacob Davies especially was ridiculed in the press for waxing lyrical about the play: 'The translation was splendidly smooth on the tongue and the dramatist's wickedly irrational dialogue hit us right between the eyes. This is indeed a gem and it should be shared with the whole of Wales by televising it and that, I would suggest, by the small company of students who showed that they really know what acting is.'[18]

According to Dafydd Glyn Jones, *Y Ffynnon* was a rather regrettable piece of mischief. No doubt this was largely the case, but the proximity of this pseudo-work to *Poen yn y Bol* is significant: in both cases, Gwenlyn managed to draw some lively theatrical expression from relatively unconventional material. Indeed, Gareth Miles recently went as far as to suggest that *Y Ffynnon* could have been a pivotal moment in the development of his writing style, exerting a significant and lasting effect on him as a dramatist. It proved to him that he could write a performable play 'without bothering about plot, characterization, period, location, structure nor beginning-middle-and-ending.'[19]

Had *Poen yn y Bol* been the last of Parry's short plays, there might be greater credibility to Miles's assessment; but, as it is, it points to a general tendency which was to come in his work, but which had not yet been realized. For the National Eisteddfod at Swansea in 1964, he submitted two short plays: the first, a supernatural comedy for children entitled *Perla' Siwan*; and the second, *Hwyr a Bore*, which was jointly successful in the original short play competition and became the third of his works to be included in his published collection *Tair Drama Fer* ['Three short plays'], in 1965.

Perla' Siwan ['Siwan's pearls']
(unpublished; 1964)

This is a very basic three-scene intrigue play, in which a robbery is planned but is foiled by an unexpected intervention. In a Welsh stately home, Ifans, a gardener, and his accomplice Meri the maid have made a pact to share the spoils gained by robbing Lady Iris of her valuable pearls. However, their plans are suddenly complicated by the unexpected return of Lady Iris's children, Alun and Sian, and their friends Twm and Luned. Later, Lady Iris tells the children a story about the curse cast on her pearls and of the horrible fate which awaits anyone who should steal them. Two such instances are recounted, the second of which occurred thirty years before (to the very night), and which Ifans claims to remember. He warns the children to stay away from the sitting-room that night; but Twm hatches a plan to frighten the sceptical Luned by dressing up as ghosts of the dead victims of the curse.

At midnight, both the robbery and the children's prank are enacted simultaneously, with predictable results: the children ambush the thieving servants rather than Luned, and thus foil the crime. There follows a dramatic twist when Ifans is discovered, dead, having been strangled by the very pearls which he tried to steal (this, of course, being precisely the fate which befell the previous thief, thirty years before; and Alun discovers that he was assisted in his ambush not by his friend Twm but by a real ghost.

Little more need be said about this play; it is a standard piece of cheery amateur drama, and interesting only as a departure from the kind of work which one might expect of Parry.

Hwyr a Bore ['Evening and morning'] (1964)

The action is set in a small quarrying town in north Wales in a family house containing William and Cadi Parri, and their two children, Dic and Marged. It takes place on a day which, co-incidentally, marks the beginning of William's retirement from quarrying and his son Dic's first day at work in a draper's shop. Cadi, who rules the roost, is at her wits' end, preparing breakfast for her son and simultaneously trying to dispose of the detritus of her husband's former life as a quarryman. William offers Dic his battered old food tin to go to the shop; Dic, somewhat reluctantly, refuses his father's kindness because, in the social expectations associated with the draper's, such an uncouth object would not be fitting. He does, however, accept his father's belt rather than the braces which his mother has provided for him.

Scene Two takes place at the end of the working day. William has spent his time preoccupied with an accident at the quarry. Dic returns, late, and seemingly in a state of depression. He deflects the family's eager questions about his first day before revealing that he has already resigned his post at Huws the Draper's – having told the proprietor to 'stuff his bloody job' – and spent his day up at the quarry, where he will commence full-time employment the following Monday morning. William joyously presents the boy with his old boots to wear: Cadi, although greatly annoyed, accepts his decision to resign, but will not have him wearing his father's old boots – she will buy him a new pair.

It may be the fact that *Hwyr a Bore* was written for competition that accounts for its quite conventional naturalistic style. However, although considerably less playful and experimental than *Poen yn y Bol*, and although it deploys many of the preferred devices of amateur drama, it is a deceptively well-crafted short play. It is also interesting for its unapologetic use of Parry's own family as characters. Just how close he got is evident by simply examining their names: William and Marged are named directly after Gwenlyn's own father and sister; Cadi, the matriarch, is a cymricization of Katie; and it was as 'Dic' that Gwenlyn was addressed by his mother for many years. They also share a number of the major features of Parry's own family: William is a quiet, unassuming man who values the comradeship of manual labour, and has learnt how to exist in the gaps between his wife's abiding interests; Cadi is the undoubted queen of the hearth, an anxious busybody, insisting on the virtues of order and upward mobility; Marged and Dic accept their mother's authority, but both seem to have a greater degree of natural empathy for their father.

The autobiographical dimension of *Hwyr a Bore* means that there is a sense of the grotesque about the play, one which is more restrained than *Poen yn y Bol* but which is significant nonetheless. This is particularly true in the portrayal of Cadi, the mother: she is an anxious, domineering woman, reminiscent (albeit in a far more realistic way) of the grotesque mother figure in the previous play, Mam Bili. She attempts to exert control over her family and to feminize her surroundings by disposing of those objects which symbolize her husband's life as a quarryman and replacing them with ones which have a comparative delicacy about them – William's quarry boots are binned, and his best shoes placed by the fender for him to wear. This enforced femininity is associated with an aspiration to a higher social class. She is thrilled at the prospect of seeing her son work at the draper's, and has provided him with a small plastic lunchbox (in contrast to William's battered quarry tin) and a pair of braces (unlike his father's belt). Her entirely unyielding attempt to have things her own way provides the play's comic conflict and energy; but she is a deeply unsympathetic character, and her portrayal seems to be as much a matter of catharsis as of naturalistic observation. It is not until the second half of Scene Two that Cadi's anxieties are given any sort of credit: there, we realize that her middle-class aspirations are related to her fears for the safety of her husband and son. After seeing the ambulance pass the house earlier in the afternoon, she voices her relief that both William and Dic were well away from the quarry's 'claws'.[20] This justification gives the audience its first real clue that her delight in the trappings of her son's first day at work in the draper's is motivated by more than mere vanity.

By contrast, the portrayal of William is far more sympathetic, but with a kind of exasperation too at his inability to shake off his wife's yoke. Placed against his wife's fussiness in the opening scene, with her preference for the rather genteel, smug propriety of the draper's shop, the directness of the quarryman's manner seems refreshingly straightforward. He comes onto the stage having thrown a glass of water over his son in order to raise him from his bed, and proceeds to make himself a cup of tea in his old quarry mug; the dust and debris caked solidly around its handle denotes the rougher, bolder tastes of working-class masculinity and suggests a nostalgia for the honesty of that way of life, in spite of its physical dangers and humiliating initiation rites. It is no real surprise that Dic returns from his first day at work to declare that he has left the draper's and that he is determined to be a quarryman.

Parry himself, of course, did not perform the same U-turn as his namesake in the play. By the time he wrote *Hwyr a Bore*, he had left behind his earlier way of life, both socially and professionally; moreover, it must be remembered that the quarrying industry was in deep decline and Dinorwic itself was within five years of closure. But, clearly, a part of him wished that it could have been possible to follow his father's example more directly. He had tried – and was trying here – to reassert the link between himself and his father through the fantasy of theatre; and was trying to compensate himself for the feeling that, in leaving those things behind him, he had somehow been disloyal. This is what is at stake in the dialogues between Dic and William (and for that matter between Marged and her father) during the play, and particularly in the moments of unspoken understanding between the children and their father. William reveals a secret to his son when he presents him with his quarry belt (which Dic prefers to the braces which Cadi has bought him), showing him the special pockets it has inside it for hiding *celc* – small amounts of money to be discreetly retained and saved. This, in turn, prompts the son to invite his father to recommend the life of a quarryman to him. William, against his deeper wishes, declines to do so:

> DIC: (*Taking his braces off*) You'd rather see me go to the quarry wouldn't you, Tada? (*He stuffs the braces away out of sight under a cushion on one of the chairs.*)
> WILLIAM: (*Without much conviction*) Good grief, no I wouldn't. Your mother is absolutely right to send you to that shop.[21]

In a comparatively simplistic little comedy, this is quite a profound moment. William cannot expressly *tell* Dic to go to work in the quarry, because the boy has to seize that male role for himself; but fatherly approval is, like the *celc* pocket, available to him if he chooses to acknowledge it. Gwenlyn was using theatre in precisely the same way, and was allowing it to make up for the comparative silence of his own father and the overarching control of his mother by giving this father's silence far greater significance. It is on this basis that he deflects William's authority into symbolism, expressed wordlessly through stage objects. Apart from the belt, the quarry boots are probably the most important such objects, and articulate the view that William's lifetime employment has bestowed a power upon him which is beyond his wife's influence. Cadi pratfalls comically over them towards the beginning of the play, and this not only provides a motivation to throw them in the bin, it also announces William himself and his residual masculine authority. Like the other quarry objects, they are indices of his power, Freudian phalluses; and her attempt to throw them out and replace them with the decorous but functionally useless Sunday best pair constitutes an attempted castration.

Parry resolves the power struggle by means of a comic volte-face at the end of the play. The struggle between William and Cadi moves into a new phase which, although different in terms of the content of the argument, shows every sign of being the same in terms of its form. William, in quiet triumph, presents Dic with the boots which he has retrieved from the bin. Cadi, who has been temporarily defeated by Dic's defiance of her desire to draw the menfolk away from the quarry (she warns him wearily that he will regret his decision to his very soul), suddenly revives and decisively blocks her husband, pushing him out of the back door with a new resolve:

CADI: He won't be putting those things on his feet. If he has to go to work in that hole, I'll buy him a new pair.[22]

This final circularity sums up one of the main preoccupations of the early plays. It suggests how Parry was troubled and fascinated by the seemingly willed self-emasculation to which his father's home life – and possibly also his allegiance to the quarry – consigned him. He was alternately impressed by William John's acquiescence and enraged by its retreat from action. This is expressed in *Hwyr a Bore* as a conflict between a broadly Freudian notion of the paternal, which is the realm of fear and of the subject's castration, and the father as a man engaged in a conventional, lived relationship with his son. The conflict between these two experiences played an important role in Gwenlyn's early work – as we have seen, two of his first three plays referred directly to his father's experiences, either as a soldier or a quarryman; and that conflict within Parry's sense of the paternal was to continue through his next two, full-length, plays. These short apprentice pieces had also given him an opportunity to develop his own kind of dramatic voice, and it is deeply significant that he chose to do so by directly dramatizing aspects of his own life: this, too, would be an ongoing tendency in his mature work.

3

'A kind of self-therapy': *Saer Doliau*

Parry's various successes as a writer of short plays, his involvement with Theatr Fach Eryri, and his continued presence among the Tuesday night crowd at the Newborough, all encouraged him to persevere with his writing for the theatre. The most consistent influence on him and advocate of his work during this period, however, was his fellow dramatist and teacher Huw Lloyd Edwards. Edwards's support and encouragement was crucial; and he came with a good deal of credibility at the beginning of the 1960s. He had already come into his own as a dramatist, having attracted considerable critical attention since 1956 with his groundbreaking play about apartheid, *Ar Ddu a Gwyn* ['On black and white'], and his innovative but rather moralistic Pirandellian fantasy, *Cyfyng-Gyngor* ['A dilemma'] of 1958, which won the National Eisteddfod prize at Ebbw Vale. He now acted as something of a theatrical father figure to Parry: he was well-versed in the classical tradition, and, true to his vocation as a teacher, actively schooled his younger colleague in the finer points of dramaturgy and theatrical aesthetics. Gwenlyn was only too happy to reciprocate his interest; and he and Joye were soon firm friends of Lloyd Edwards and his own wife, Jane. However, much as he might have needed a model at the beginning of his writing career, someone or something to emulate in shaping his dramatic dialogue, Huw Lloyd Edwards was not it. He was considerably older than Gwenlyn, and, as William R. Lewis has suggested, had been deeply influenced by Saunders Lewis's move to contemporary international subject matter in the mid-1950s; Lloyd Edwards had tried to override much of his inherent playfulness in order to emulate the seriousness of the great man.[1] The result was a rather ostentatious rhetoric and a dry earnestness, which has not helped their historical reputation. Parry's own writing, after a somewhat unpromising beginning, had been far less heavy in its tone, and had veiled its more serious material behind a pacy black comedy or a superficial realism. He was becoming increasingly adept at creating material which spoke far more powerfully in a theatrical context than it did on the page, thanks to the counterpoint between directly evident devices (those in the characters' dialogue, for example) and more indirect ones (those which arose from the cumulative effect of textual rhythm or visual stage imagery).

The striking of such a balance did not happen by itself. Once he had begun to establish himself as a writer, as Joye Evans Parry has noted, he was never happy unless he had a pencil in his hand: 'once he began to write, the idea would come to him in a great rush, and he could barely get it all down quickly enough'.[2] Conversely, however, he was also an almost manic editor of his own work, and Joye once commented wryly that she would have to threaten to take his draft away from him: 'he would cut the story and the dialogue down to the bone until I sometimes felt that there would be nothing left. He was a terribly stern critic of his own work.'[3] Indeed, Gwenlyn himself joked about this, noting that, even though 'an untidy man with my clothes, . . . with my car, with the garden', he was 'terribly particular with a script'.[4] Unlike his colleague Rhydderch Jones, he was a confirmed grafter, and the dual aspect of his craft as a writer – free creative energy and harsh self-regulation – seems to have been in keeping with the dual nature of his personality. Be that as it may, changes in his professional life in the mid-1960s were about to ensure that he would spend a good deal of his time practising that regulation and control over his work, and that of others, in a completely new environment.

His job as a science teacher at Dyffryn Ogwen school had provided him with a means to return to Wales, a steady income and, curiously, an opportunity to sustain and influence his feeling for theatricality. Presenting experiments in the lab, he said, had a sense of showmanship and focused spectatorship to it: 'there was something exciting about . . . looking at something taking place – an experiment, all eyes on the experiment'.[5] His teaching post also gave him a chance to support dramatic activity at the school. He assumed responsibility for the production of school plays, which featured a number of budding actors who would soon find themselves treading the boards of the professional stage in Wales – the most precocious being John Ogwen, who would become closely associated with some of Gwenlyn's most important works for stage and television. But his dedication to writing and producing drama was becoming an ever more prevalent part of his life. By 1964, along with Rhydderch, he was part of a team of writers scripting sketches and other pieces for a popular weekly BBC satirical magazine programme, *Stiwdio B* (a kind of Welsh counterpart to the groundbreaking *TW3*), produced by Meredydd Evans at the BBC Light Entertainment Department in Cardiff; he was also engaged as a Saturday morning radio presenter. The success of *Stiwdio B* led to further interest from the BBC. In 1965, he was contacted by Wilbert Lloyd Roberts, the Head of the BBC Drama Department in Bangor, and offered a one-year contract as a script editor. Rhydderch had already left his teaching job at Llanrwst in order to join the BBC Light Entertainment Department, and Parry felt no little envy at his friend's new opportunity. But, although supported by his wife Joye, the idea of giving up his nominated career caused him some trepidation, too. Among other things, like Dic in *Hwyr a Bore*, he would have to face down his mother: 'Mam wanted me to be a minister or a teacher, she never mentioned being a writer'.[6] But he knew his own mind, and could not allow himself to sit 'for the rest of my life in a noisy classroom or a smoky staff room dreaming of the opportunity that had passed me by.'[7] He took up his new post in January 1966.

It was probably the most momentous decision of his life. However, to a considerable extent, it was one which he had already precipitated by his decision to embark on a project which would consume his energies and bring him to the attention of the Welsh public as a whole: his first full-length play, *Saer Doliau*.

Saer Doliau ['Doll doctor'] (1966)

In 1963, the playwright W. S. Jones and his brother Elis Gwyn, who ran the little Theatr y Gegin in Cricieth, produced *Y Gofalwr*, a Welsh version of Harold Pinter's *The Caretaker*. It is a mark of Theatr y Gegin's ambition and faith in its local audience that it should have attempted a piece whose theatricality was so delicate and which required such crafted ensemble playing; and such was the success of Elis Gwyn's remarkable translation that it created a highly successful production, and was later taken up by Cwmni Theatr Cymru in 1970, and then again by Theatr Genedlaethol Cymru in 2008. Emboldened by *Y Gofalwr*, Theatr y Gegin commissioned Parry to write a play which was to function as a showpiece for Guto Roberts, who had played Davies in *Y Gofalwr*, and one of Theatr y Gegin's best-known actors. Theatr y Gegin's production foundered, however, and *Saer Doliau*, drafted but by no means completed, was left without a means of production. It was at this point that Wilbert Lloyd Roberts – in his other capacity as artistic director of Cwmni Theatr Cymru, the Welsh language arm of the professional Welsh Theatre Company – stepped in to develop and produce the play. Theatr Cymru was still in its early days, and Lloyd Roberts was extremely keen to establish its reputation and independence by staging new work. A newly completed draft of a full-length play by a promising young dramatist was just what he had been seeking.

With *Saer Doliau*, Parry was writing a play outside the remit of competition for the first time. This brought with it some problems, because – as already noted – he liked to write to a prescribed brief or to a pre-existing model. Theatr y Gegin's commission had helped to a certain extent in defining the kind of play which he could produce, and the idea of creating some kind of continuity with their production of Pinter's *Y Gofalwr* served to suggest a framework and a context for his efforts. But he was on unfamiliar territory, and it is hardly a surprise that the play, throughout the period of 'two or three years' which it took to write, grew to give theatrical form to what he called 'the anguish of losing faith'.[8] With this full-length work, he was facing some fundamental questions about himself as a writer and as a man, and, even if limited by an external brief, was determined to make his work follow a form dictated by the release of his imagination.

This crisis of faith was not new. By his own admission, he had seriously questioned the existence of God at the age of eighteen, but an implicit Christianity had persisted in him, hard-wired into his being by his upbringing and by his cultural environment. Now, however, the idea of faith reasserted itself in his life in a radically different form as a result of reading *Honest to God* by John A. T. Robinson, Bishop of Woolwich, in 1963. This book, particularly after being publicized by an interview in *The Observer* newspaper, had created a great stir among believers of all kinds by bringing the existential theology of Paul Tillich, Dietrich Bonhoeffer and Rudolf Bultmann to a surprisingly wide audience. It argued for a radical reappraisal of some of the basic approaches to the Christian faith, with Robinson committed to overthrowing the traditional idea of a God who existed 'up there' or 'out there'. God, he contended, had to be understood and experienced 'in here', within the immediate experience of an individual's existence rather than through traditional iconography or the trappings of formalized worship. Parry was mesmerized:

> our original ideas, the ones I had adopted in Sunday School about God were completely wrong – completely mad – he said that 'there is no such thing as the old man in the sky' – . . . and I had thought of God as a kind of old man in the sky with a beard looking down at his register, adding a red mark, a black mark.[9]

Saer Doliau thus coincided with Parry's reappraisal of his spiritual and intellectual upbringing, and became a response to the re-articulation of the idea of God in Robinson's work.[10] What was most powerful about the book from Gwenlyn's point of view was the internalization of the presence of God and the concomitant shift in terms of the language and imagery which was appropriate to describe it. God was no longer subject to that common vocabulary of religious experience which Parry had acquired during his childhood, and had enjoyed largely as a form of performance; He was now as vital and as immediate as the very poetic language through which Parry was attempting to define and carry out his vocation as an artist. He *was* that language.

The play sees the *Saer* or mender of dolls, Effraim Cadwaladr Ifans, interrupted in his workshop one morning by the arrival of a mysterious Girl who, it appears, has come to inspect his working practices and the efficiency of his operation. It is not made clear who has sent her, and the *Saer* himself is so shaken by her arrival that he forgets to ask. Very soon, she has introduced a Lad to him, who will work as his apprentice. The *Saer*, troubled by this interference in his business, attempts to contact the *Giaffar* – the (absent) manager – via the workshop telephone. The Girl declares that the whole operation should be modernized, and that electronically-powered machinery should be introduced into the workshop. This pleases the Lad, but appals the *Saer*, who decides to destroy the new equipment. However, his declaration of war against the new order (made over the phone to the *Giaffar*) is overheard, and he is ambushed in the act of sabotage by the Girl and the Lad; they create a scenario in which the machines appear to have acquired a life of their own and turned against him. The *Saer* is not fooled by their attempt to frighten him but, wearied by it all, turns to the *Giaffar* for support. He is then told by the Lad that the telephone line is completely useless, connected to nothing except 'a cobweb on the ceiling'. The cellar door swings open, and Ifans, suddenly seized as if by a demon and unable to escape the workshop, promptly dies of fright. The Girl exits, leaving the Lad to clear away the *Saer*'s body and assume his role as 'doll doctor'. Left alone in the workshop, he is suddenly disturbed by the ringing of the supposedly disconnected telephone.

Famously, the idea for 'something like *Saer Doliau*' came to Parry as he was standing in a branch of Woolworths in Bangor. He saw the rows of dolls stacked on shelves 'sitting there, staring', and thought that 'this would be a great theatrical experience'.[11] But, in the process of writing, the play soon began to generate a momentum and a 'mind' of its own, which he described in an interview:

I noticed that there were metaphors which offered themselves up – the carpenter's workshop, the carpenter, religious metaphors perhaps . . . it insisted on coming to the surface in *Saer Doliau* . . . [it was] a kind of self-therapy in the end, during the process of writing, some kind of attempt to answer the questions which are troubling you . . . The play grew during its writing to address my experience of losing faith.[12]

Parry's description of the process of writing as 'therapy' is significant: he applied it very generally to his work as a dramatist thereafter, in particular to the unbidden and unforeseeable intercession of what he described as images from the subconscious.[13] Writing *Saer Doliau*, he found himself engaged in a flow of words, ideas and images (in Freudian terms, a cathexis), an essentially dynamic action, in which he could not 'pretend to know the answers in advance'; and in which writing was 'much more a matter of sensing certain things on the pulses, of groping forward, almost of being pushed from behind; and of following the argument wherever it led', as John A. T. Robinson himself had noted in relation to the writing of *Honest to God*.[14] However, as a work of theatre, *Saer Doliau* is not just a matter of flow. It is not just an examination of the issue of his faith: it is also an observation of that examination. During the process of writing, Parry was confronted by the characters, situations and images which he was producing. They stared back at him, as it were, and he observed them engaging him in dialogue. And so the action of the play does not merely constitute a 'therapy' in terms of catharsis, it is also a conversation with himself, and with his sense of what it is to be an audience.

From the very beginning, the play emphasizes the importance of looking and observing. Even before the action begins, we are faced with a room full of dolls, arranged, like the audience itself, in rows and ranks, staring intently ahead. The situation is already metatheatrical, and Ifans the *Saer* only accentuates this on entry by being self-consciously performative. He refers to himself in the third person, and adopts the language trope of a teacher: 'Good morning, children. How was the night for you? Mh? Everyone slept well? Or were you disturbed. Don't worry, old Ifans is here again to mend you and to look after you.'[15] He is indulging in a fantasy, in which he ascribes sentient life to his inanimate charges, and through which his own authority is rendered unimpeachable. But the fragility of this fantasy, and its function as a form of denial, is immediately evident to the audience. The workshop is in disarray, and the unblinking stare of the dolls seems to incriminate Ifans for his wilful blindness to this fact.

The personal consequences of his denial are quickly made apparent. Dismayed by the delivery of a parcel of black dolls, which he disparagingly (and from a contemporary point of view, disappointingly) refers to as *'petha caridyms'* – a distinctly Arfonian expression meaning 'worthless things' – he throws them down into the cellar, in an act of evacuation which clearly brings him some relief. But, as a result of this action, the cellar becomes a tainted place, one which, to the *Saer's* mind, houses an invisible but implacable enemy: *'Y Fo'* ['him']. This creature, he says, frustrates him at every turn, mocking him by stealing or hiding his tools, prowling through the workshop at night by walking through the walls. *Y Fo* is at his most active when Ifans is unaware or absent, and thus unable to exert control over the situation through the playing out of his role as *Saer*. *Y Fo* is, in effect, watching him at every turn. The existence of this threatening persona clearly necessitates the creation of a counteracting agency, the *Giaffar*, whom Ifans telephones in order to 'tell' on *Y Fo* and to reassert his management of the workshop. For many critics, Dewi Z. Phillips most particularly perhaps, the implied duologue between Ifans and the *Giaffar* equates to the act of prayer, with Ifans talking earnestly to a presence that he (and we) cannot see or hear, nor fully envisage. He does not communicate in traditional religious language, but this, Phillips argues, does not corrupt the essence of the act since he brings his cares, his fears and desires to the call, without questioning how or even whether his communication with the *Giaffar* might help him.

In that respect, Phillips's view is quite correct. But the idea that this scene correlates directly with the act of prayer is problematic. For all its intimacy, prayer does not generally involve fully-fledged dialogue; and in this first exchange, it does appear that Ifans and the *Giaffar* are engaged in a conversation. More importantly, in the sense in which Phillips argues his case in *Dramâu Gwenlyn Parry*, there can be no understanding of or access to the act of prayer except through the act of prayer itself. The audience thus cannot witness prayer, only a man praying: as viewers of the representation, we cannot access the experience. The *Giaffar* is present to us merely as a projection through Ifans's (possibly fanciful) engagement with him and via his ascription of authority to him. Once again, the act of *looking* plays a crucial role in defining, and, in this case, constraining the action. What we do witness is Ifans inventing and animating the *Giaffar* through conversational language, and implementing his authority as an ego-ideal to counteract the vile capriciousness and malignity of *Y Fo* in the cellar. The fact that Ifans lies to the *Giaffar* (and thus to himself) about the state of the workshop, means that he is fundamentally at odds with the ego-ideal; but he needs it, and his access to the higher function which it represents, in order to sustain himself.

The act of looking takes on a different form when the Girl appears. She is an alien presence, who does not reveal the purpose of her appearance in the workshop until the end of Scene One, and up to that point acts as a kind of mirror. In a comically convoluted passage, she attracts the *Saer*'s sexual interest but then deflects or denies it, using his responses as a prompt for her own. When she does describe herself to him, she uses expressions which are consistent with the idea of a reflection in a mirror: she will be 'Like the things . . . that are with you day and night that you cannot touch or drive away.'[16] The Girl's inconsistency and evasiveness created problems for some of the play's original audience members. Aneirin Talfan Davies, in his preface to the published edition of the play, complained that she was 'too much of a symbol'. Of what, he was not sure: '(Eve? Time?)'.[17] But his view of her identity as symbolic is simply a product of Parry's refusal to contextualize her appearance and to describe her function: she is, in fact, no more a symbol than any of the other characters. Rather, she is a theatrical intermediary, a disengaged viewer. We are given a hint of this in her first line:

IFANS: Hey! Hey, you there. What do you think you're doing?
GIRL: Nothing. I'm doing nothing. I am looking.[18]

Her assertion that she is 'doing nothing . . . looking', suggests, paradoxically, that she *is* doing something. In fact, she is doing precisely the same thing that the dolls on stage seem to be doing and that the audience in the auditorium is doing. They are silently consuming the spectacle of the *Saer*'s bumbling ineffectiveness for their own entertainment, and suspending a reaction. Moreover, if we take the Girl's words at their face value, she personifies the act of looking: 'I am looking', she says.[19] Dewi Z. Phillips is thus quite correct when identifying her as a figure who equates to notions of positivism and materiality: she is there in order to alienate *us* from the theatrical event, and to try to embody a disconnected position.

The play develops, then, as a conflict between the *Saer*'s quasi-primitive identification with his environment (which produces *Y Fo* and the *Giaffar*) and the Girl's quasi-scientific objectification of it. It also perpetuates the conflict between paternal and maternal roles as seen already, satirically, in *Hwyr a Bore* and *Poen yn y Bol*. The *Giaffar* encompasses the paternal/fatherly role, an authoritative but curiously inert figure, while the Girl is the one who wields real power, albeit of a deterministic and destructive kind. Here, as in previous plays – and in a good number of Parry's works to come – the paternal male is the subject through which the action of the play is experienced, while the female is the object, the 'other', who brings the excitation of conflict to the self-sustaining but insubstantial world of individual fantasy.

From this set-up, the play proceeds through intrigue to its conclusion. The Lad is introduced as a comparatively mindless youngster, a biddable puppet-doll of the Girl's making who stands outside the *Saer*'s fantasy. But, being a male character, he quickly begins to adopt some of the traits of his older male counterpart. Though he rejects the existence of the *Giaffar* as a nonsense, he tacitly accepts his presence at the other end of the phone line: when he fears that he is being misrepresented as a layabout by the *Saer*, for example, he tries to protest his innocence to the 'Chief' while Ifans fights to deny him access to the phone; and even after the Girl has suggested to him that the phone is disconnected, and that Ifans is merely talking to himself when he converses with the *Giaffar*, the Lad – when left on his own – is still fascinated enough to try talking down the phone line. Similarly, though he dismisses the notion that there is something living in the cellar, even to the point of sarcastically goading *Y Fo* in order to provoke and humiliate Ifans, the Lad later becomes a kind of personification of it when he emerges from the storeroom wearing his depersonalizing motor-cycle gear and crash helmet. These things obscure his face and identity; and though he mocks the idea that he is the '*Bwci*' from the cellar, the audience have been made to experience the strange-ness of his emergence from the darkness precisely as that kind of spectre. On a conscious level, we may know very well that he is not *Y Fo*; but in creating stage imagery, the play does not address the act of looking on a conscious level alone.

After Ifans has died, the Lad becomes a different kind of 'spectre' by acquiring the identity of the *Saer*, an induction into subjective fantasy which is crowned by the ringing of the telephone. It is this final moment, this last device in the play, which has lingered in the imagination of generations of Welsh theatregoers. The ringing of the telephone reasserts the possibility of the *Giaffar's* existence and has been regarded ever since as one of the high points of Parry's drama, a masterful *coup de théâtre*. But it had not been included in the original draft of the play. Gwenlyn had been stuck for an ending, and was reportedly dissatisfied with the play's downbeat con-clusion. The ringing telephone was added at a late stage of the rehearsal process, as indicated by press reports immediately pre-ceding the production. Describing *Saer Doliau* as a 'completely new form of drama', these noted that the novel aspect of the experience was the fact that the play could end 'in more than one way', and that it would 'not be decided until a short time before the first performance in which way this would be done'. More significantly, perhaps, is the fact that the play was labelled as 'a project' arising from the ideas and input of the dramatist, the director and the actors.[20] Whoever suggested the ringing telephone – and its invention has been ascribed to a number of different individuals – the device is ultimately Gwenlyn's: he, after all, had to accept the suggestion and incorporate it into the script. Nonetheless, it is instructive that this most famous moment – arguably the most famous moment in twentieth-century Welsh drama – had not been originally envisaged by the dramatist himself.

For all its fame as a device, a number of critics have argued that it is superfluous. Certainly, it does not necessarily follow the dramatic logic of the play. The action has already been completed by the Lad's tacit acceptance of the role of *Saer* following Ifans's death. In that sense, there is no need for the phone to ring. But this is where the underlying potency of Gwenlyn's theatrical vision comes to the fore, and will not be denied. As Dewi Z. Phillips noted in reappraising his view of the play in 1995, the power of the device has to be respected in its own right. In relation to the logic of the drama, it is not possible for the phone to ring – it is not connected to anything. 'But what if it rang in spite of this?', asks Phillips.[21] The very lack of an explanation leaves the audience with that which is most true to the action: a question.

In favouring the impossible at the end of his play, Parry was establishing a notion which subsequently informed the entirety of his practice as a playwright: the fact that the 'logic' of theatre is quite different from that of drama. Whereas drama (put very simply) involves the conceptual proposition of character, situation and action, theatre involves the active manifestation of those things, *transformed*, before the eyes of an audience. It is a medium which, at every moment, enacts the miraculous. The ringing of the telephone at the end of *Saer Doliau* was just a final reminder of this. Similarly, the intelligence which Parry brought to this play was not schematic ('allegorical', as a number of critics argued at the time) but intuitive – 'therapeutical', to apply his own term – and was typified by the fact that, at the last, he was prepared to trust others to come up with his punchline.

Whatever Parry's hopes for *Saer Doliau* may have been, it proved to be his entrée into the national consciousness of Welsh-speaking Wales. He had arrived, and in no uncertain terms. Although there was a good deal of discussion about the meaning of the play after its first performances in April 1966, very few reviewers and critics at the time dissented from the view that this was a play, and a playwright, of considerable stature. Its originality was a key factor in this (the dramatist 'keeps his audience in confusion the whole time, giving them freedom to interpret the symbols as they wish',[22] marvelled Eleanor Dwyryd), but the nature of the presentation was also crucial. For all Theatr y Gegin's buoyant originality as a company, Gwenlyn was singularly fortunate that the play had been taken up by Cwmni Theatr Cymru. As Meic Povey has noted, the sheer scale of Cwmni Theatr Cymru's production, its visual impact and the compelling performance of David Lyn as Ifans set it apart from a great deal of Welsh-language theatre at the time. It was revived, after 'dozens of requests for this to happen', at the Aberafan National Eisteddfod in August (alongside – and much to Parry's delight – *Pros Kairon* by Huw Lloyd Edwards).[23]

It was avidly discussed, keeping one commentator and his friends up into the small hours of the morning, 'arguing passionately about its meaning, and none of us would dare say that they understood the significance of all the symbols even now'.[24] To the television critic J. S. Williams, it was a conflict not just between 'one generation and another', but between 'the Children of Ptolemy and the Children of Copernicus';[25] to the journalist Frank Price Jones, its tension was like one of the sermons of the nineteenth-century 'Pope of Anglesey', John Elias;[26] and to the poet Gwilym R. Tilsley and his (very eminent) friends, its basic situation alluded to a range of possible religious interpretations:

> On the way out I discussed the play briefly with Gwilym R., Mathonwy, Kate Roberts and others and everyone agreed that it was a stunner of a play – the best by a Welsh playwright that she had ever seen, said K. R . . .
> The workshop was the Church, said Gwilym R., where souls are so untidily mended. But K. R. and I felt that the workshop was this life and that the dolls represented all the acts of man . . . The thing that brought us great relief (all old religionists at heart!) was the ringing of the phone at the end. This was a masterstroke.[27]

It had become public property, one of the main cultural events of the year, inspiring articles, discussions, sermons and even a satirical short story called '*Saer Cyboliau*' ['The maker of excuses'], published in *Barn* magazine in November, in which a discussion of *Saer Doliau* leads to an inflammatory power struggle between a man and wife.[28] The business of trying to disentangle the meaning of the play, to clarify its many ambiguities – as if to discover and explain what the playwright was really trying to say – fascinated and baffled many. Gwenlyn was, accordingly, pressed for answers. But his response at the time was – to say the least – somewhat coy. On the television discussion programme *Disgwyl Cwmni* ['Expecting company'], he was 'provocatively cautious about explaining the meaning of and interpreting the play. Very modestly, all he was concerned about was that this play should give two hours of pleasure to its audience.'[29] And when, urged by the crowd, and egged on by the director Wilbert Lloyd Roberts, to ascend the stage after a production of *Saer Doliau* at the Cyncoed teacher training college in Cardiff, Gwenlyn remained firmly seated. He could not yet to allow himself to accept the kind of public approbation which his play, suddenly, appeared to be conferring upon him.[30]

4

'A revolution . . .where one man takes over the empire of the other': *Tŷ ar y Tywod*

The same reticence, it seemed, was still in evidence in 1969 in the introduction to the published version of his next play, *Tŷ ar y Tywod*. Those seeking clarification of the thematic context of *Saer Doliau* and a pointer to the meaning of his new work would have been disappointed: Gwenlyn remained thoroughly inscrutable. 'I have been asked to say a word or two at the outset about *Tŷ ar y Tywod*,' he noted, 'but I won't. I do not think that an author should try to analyse or explain his own work lest he, by so doing, should condition his audience's minds.'[1] His refusal to plead may have been prompted by John Rowlands's scathing critique of *Saer Doliau* in *Y Traethodydd* in October 1968. Rowlands criticized the play for its superficial absorption of the ideas and principles of the Absurd: 'this is a play which has borrowed some of the external aspects of Absurd drama without taking on its point of view. In a word, what we have here is a *masquerade* of Absurd drama.'[2] *Saer Doliau* was, by his reckoning, aspiring to Pinter's 'comedy of menace', but with little finesse in its 'rambling' dialogue, and with 'overly obvious' symbolism throughout. Parry, he said, was kowtowing to the most basic audience expectations, and it would have been better 'if he had more faith in his audience than that.'[3]

Rowlands's critique, although harshly expressed, was quite valid in many ways. Parry had chosen to adopt certain characteristics of the Absurd – particularly as manifested in the work of Harold Pinter (and perhaps particularly as in *The Caretaker* and *The Dumb Waiter*) – without embracing the full implications of Absurdism as a view of the world. He had done so because he was not an Absurd-ist writer at heart, and *Saer Doliau* was not an Absurdist play. As a drama, it was a condensed tragicomedy, but, crucially, one whose gently reductive sense of loss was confounded at the last by a grand moment of contradiction: the ringing of the telephone. While this had certainly been a concession to those 'old religionists at heart' who were still a vital constituency for Welsh theatre, it could hardly be said to indicate a lack of faith in his audience. It required the audience to accept that the theatricality of the play was meaningful in itself, that the action – like John A. T. Robinson's description of contemporary Christian belief – was dynamic, immediate, and more significant in its (subconscious) continuity rather than its resultant imagery. Articulating this almost unnameable sense of a (possibly higher) intelligence within the drive to action was his fundamental purpose, and there can be little doubt, John Rowlands's objections notwithstanding, that he succeeded.

He tried to develop this idea in his introduction to *Tŷ ar y Tywod*, where he argued that the significance of his play lay in the immediate moment of its theatrical exposure rather than in the programmatic nature of its content: 'you . . . have to remember that, ultimately, drama isn't something that goes on between characters on stage, but between a character on stage and a character in the audience. That is my main purpose, then – to communicate with the audience at that moment in the theatre, and to be perfectly honest, I have far more interest in appealing to their imagination than to their intellect.'[4] If this were not incitement enough for some critics, his final conclusion about his plays certainly provided them with fuel for their fires: 'If they have a message in them', he said, 'that message will be whatever the viewer sees'.[5] This statement was much discussed, seen by some as evidence that Parry was either being deliberately evasive, or indulging in rather clever analysis for the sake of it. Gwenlyn himself countered this by arguing in favour of the indeterminacy of theatrical presentation and against what he perceived as some critics' (probably John Rowlands, in this case) demand for a completed meaning:

After a performance of *Saer Doliau* I said that I had heard five different interpretations of the play, each one entirely plausible. I was criticized for saying so because there are some people who insist that there is a definite limit to the meaning of words. This may well be so, but if there is a limit to their meaning, I am perfectly sure that there is no limit to their associations.[6]

There were a number of critics who did accept Parry's work in its theatrical context. One of the most obvious was Dafydd Glyn Jones, who, reviewing the published script of *Saer Doliau* in 1968, argued that the strength of the play lay 'not in its literary suggestiveness but in its sparing theatrical self-sufficiency.'[7] And he noted his dismay at many of the vociferously literal responses to the play: 'I cannot feel but that the interpretations of it as a discussion of "the state of the Church today", or some other topic, are too narrow, too specific. They are at once burdensome and insufficient.'[8] But to move the public on from such a content-fixated interpretation was not easy. Even for some members of the Welsh *literati*, to accept theatrical presentation as inherently meaningful – to accept its dynamic flux as a reflection of a similar instability in their own condition – was a step too far. In their view, the production of a play was just a means of bringing to public life its internal conflicts as imagined by the dramatist. The job of the director and the actors was to represent those conflicts 'correctly', that is, in as lifelike a manner as possible, and as the dramatist himself would surely wish. The argument that a play could acquire an independent life for itself through production was, largely, a pretext for a dangerous self-indulgence.

The critical fallout from *Saer Doliau* is significant when discussing *Tŷ ar y Tywod*, not only because they share a number of basic formal features, but because Gwenlyn's new play was forced to operate in the shadow of its predecessor, and because *Saer Doliau*'s success acted as a kind of hidden narrative throughout. Behind its overt subject matter, *Tŷ ar y Tywod* is about being accepted into a new world, and allowing that new world to re-shape you. In Parry's case, the 'new world' was public recognition, from which he had shied away at the time of *Saer Doliau*'s staging two years previously, but which was now his accepted professional lot. The play was commissioned by the National Eisteddfod of Wales for presentation by Cwmni Theatr Cymru at Barry in 1968, and at the same time was to be produced as a television drama by the BBC for broadcast over the Christmas period. This time, success or failure could be nothing other than highly public, and he would be judged by his previous achievement. The play reflects this through its main character, the Man of the House, who – somewhat like his predecessor Ifans, and certainly like his creator Gwenlyn – is a contradictory individual, both passionate and timid (and preoccupied with images), who finds himself taking on the power of a forceful and forbidding thrill factory. As before, Parry's immediate circumstances provided him with the basic conflicts and imagery for his work.

Tŷ ar y Tywod ['A house on the sand'] (1968)

Tŷ ar y Tywod takes place in a rickety beach shack, the 'House on the Sand' of the title; and opens with the reclusive Man of the House returning home from a visit to the nearby fairground, where he has stolen a waxwork dummy of the murderess Lisa Prydderch from the Chamber of Horrors. He has adored this Dummy for some time, and now resolves to protect her, even to use his shotgun if necessary. According to Parry's own synopsis of the play, the Dummy, 'during the course of the play comes "alive" to satisfy his fantasies (he even goes through a marriage ceremony with her).'[9] He is accosted by thugs (a Boy and a Girl) sent by the Fair Owner, who accuse him of theft and of being insane. The Fair Owner himself pays a visit, and declares his intention to expand the fairground by acquiring the beach shack; but when he mishandles the Dummy, the Man of the House becomes enraged and threatens him with the shotgun. The Dummy herself urges him on throughout.

At this point, a role-reversal begins, with the increasingly desperate, and weak, Fair Owner offering an ever greater share of his fairground to the Man of the House. According to Parry, 'they interchange characters physically (by changing clothes) and mentally (by changing attitudes). The Man of the House grows in strength while the [Fair Owner] degenerates to a worthless, activeless [*sic*], speechless imbecile.'[10] The Fair Owner's thugs return, but decide to take their orders from the Man of the House, who by now not only looks like the Fair Owner but also talks like him. The transformation is completed as the Fair Owner begins to believe in his ability to communicate with the Dummy, and as the beach shack, in a dizzying whirl of lighting and sound effects, is absorbed into the fairground.

As noted, *Tŷ ar y Tywod* reiterates a number of the key devices and concerns of *Saer Doliau* (indeed, Aneirin Talfan Davies, the producer of the televised version in December 1968, told Parry that it was a shame he had 'followed up *Saer Doliau* with a play which follows the same course').[11] The similarities between the two plays are marked – and significant, considering the great difference between some of the earlier short plays: both use a single dramatic location in order to examine the theatrical potential of an enclosed situation; both portray a vulnerable and putatively innocent main character who is removed from the contemporary technocratic world and threatened by its representatives; both involve the partial animation of nominally 'dead' humanoid dolls and dummies; and so on. What is notable is that these devices and characteristics are far more overtly deployed and developed in *Tŷ ar y Tywod* than they were in its predecessor. It is a considerably less subtle and less guarded expression of his dramatic vision than *Saer Doliau*.

As if to prove and highlight this fact, one of the most important and evident characteristics of the play is its underlying Oedipal theme. The three main characters form a basic Oedipal triangle: the childlike male subject, the desired female subject/object, and the feared male object. The child, in the guise of the Man of the House, is oppressed by an aberrant father figure, and possesses both an infantilized lust and a deep desire to be restored to the affections of the maternal (both drives are directed towards the Dummy). The feared male object, the Fair Owner, does not appear in the early part of the play, but is represented instead by an imposing and rather terrifying phallic insignia, the fairground. And the female subject/object, the Dummy, or 'Lisa Prydderch', alternately accedes to and frustrates the Man's desires, defining him as both a lover and an infant in relation to her. Indeed, she constitutes the female as seen during almost every possible stage of male sexual development: she is a mother to the unborn infant in the womb, a mother to a powerless but needy child, a playmate, an adolescent fantasy figure, a girl who mocks his feelings, a lover and a wife.

During the course of the action, the weak Man overcomes his Oedipal subjection and defeats the designated object of terror, but the uncastrated energy which possesses him as a result of his emancipation is highly aggressive and destructive. He 'becomes' the Fair Owner, assertively adopting those traits with which his opponent has been associated during the play (and eventually even rejecting the notion that the Dummy is alive). On the other hand, the Fair Owner regresses to an infantile state. This climactic transformation is powerful, but it is unclear whether it constitutes a cathartic release from repression, or merely a kind of exchange, in which the fundamental roles within the Oedipal triangle remain intact even though the characters occupying each role have changed. It is a triumphant, liberated brutality but also a nightmarish continuation of the means of repression. In either case, the play remains very true to Freud's idea of Oedipality, because it does not simply reduce it to a series of metaphorical postures, but rather demonstrates its dynamic and experiential nature, presenting it as a set of forces and flows which ultimately transcend character boundaries.

Parry himself did not refer directly to the Oedipal nature of the play. In his synopsis, he described the transformation of the two male characters as 'a revolution . . . where one man takes over the empire of the other'.[12] The political inference in this interpretation is entirely appropriate for a play produced in 1968 (although it must be remembered that Parry wrote his synopsis in 1977); but the scenario of revolution in *Tŷ ar y Tywod* does not go much further than a mere initial revolt, and the 'empire' that is overthrown is far more a phallic object of terror than a political regime. It is that phallic aspect of the fairground which is responsible for defining the lead character, the Man of the House, as a grotesquely weak and introverted loner.

Like Ifans the *Saer*, he is a low-status individual given a central position in the action from the very beginning. Not only does he regale the audience with a long opening monologue, but he is also given a distinctly metatheatrical significance because he is a fantasist, prone to visions and convinced of the possibility that life exists within what could be seen as an inanimate object (the same was true in Ifans's case in relation to the dolls and the telephone). When we first see the Man, he is desperate to release the Dummy from her chains, and so to release the life within her: this is a fundamentally illogical belief, but is made credible because of the power with which theatrical representation imbues the enactment of his fantasy. He, like us, wants to believe in, and thus animate, the proposition which stands before us. His wish is fulfilled. The Dummy comes to life, and they play out a journey together to an island where he marries her. However, Parry undermines whatever happiness or delight we may take in this fantasy by the pointedly excessive nature of its fulfilment. The Man dispenses with the constraints of reality all too easily, a fact which projects his story and that of the play into the realm of fairy tale and tends to suggest that the Man's needs are infantile rather than fully mature. It is also suggested by the fact that he is enclosed within a very fragile and isolating world. To all intents and purposes, he is in a womb. His house, the beach shack, is a ramshackle affair, described as '*unreal and very fragile-looking*' with walls so insubstantial they '*could be made of cards*'.[13] His own physical state is also described as extremely – excessively – fragile, with the stage directions emphasizing that he '*cannot bear even the slightest amount of pain, and that he has a terrible fear of any kind of viciousness*'.[14] As befits one encased by a womb, he is largely unable to interact with the outside world: his poor eyesight restricts his freedom of activity and expression, and, in an obvious echo of the downtrodden Clov in Beckett's *Endgame*, he uses a telescope to observe the outside world.

The result of this vulnerability and isolation is that his view of society has become a detached, voyeuristic one. Socialization has yielded to fetishization, and the Dummy has become the focus for his most intimate feelings and desires. As a result, she has become what Žižek has called an 'an autonomous partial object' by means of which the Man fantasizes a full existence for himself (again, the same could be said of Ifans in *Saer Doliau*, again through his attachment to the telephone as well as to the miniature humanoid dolls). Although he wishes her to be alive, and poetically ascribes feelings of suffering to her ('you were only one in a crowd [. . .] a cold, lonely crowd [. . .] frozen for all time [. . .] But I saw the pain behind your still eyes [. . .] the pain and the fear'),[15] she is also, undeniably, an amenable object. While still poeticizing her silent agony, he is frantically sawing away at her chains, an action whose sexual – masturbatory – implications cannot be overlooked. She – like any number of Parry's female characters up to this point – can only be a superficial figure, an agency rather than a personality and a mere function of the Man's action.

However, as the play develops the Dummy comes to represent more than just the idyllic love-object. The Man recalls an incident 'on the day of the Carnival' when, he says, he had stared at her, seeing her as the most beautiful girl there; he had even ventured to follow her around, wishing that he could talk to her. But she rejected him: 'you turned up your nose [. . .] turned your back [. . .] laughed [. . .] oh yes, I heard you laughing with the rest as I hurried away . . . laughing and mocking'.[16] Rather like the implicitly split nature of the paternal object in *Saer Doliau* (divided between the nurturing *Giaffar* and the terrifying *Y Fo*), the Dummy's role here begins to be more than merely that of a romanticized Pinocchio. She begins to be split into, or associated with, a number of female figures, including his previous lovers, possibly even the woman he admires through the telescope as she runs down to the sea;[17] but most importantly, his mother. This is accelerated when the two fairground 'heavies' invade the shack: the horrified Man lapses into a regressive waking dream, in which he addresses a wife, the mother who has lost her baby, and a so-far nameless assailant who 'ripped the rose from her cheek [. . .] scraped the gold from her hair [. . .] treated her like an animal.'[18] This composite allusion becomes clearer as the play progresses, eventually coalescing into a triangular relationship, with the Man as a powerless child (possibly still in the womb), the Dummy as both the Man's bride and his mother and the Fair Owner as an abusive husband and father:

> MAN: But he was [. . .] you don't understand [. . .] he was . . . Cruel like an animal [. . .] like a monster . . . Shouting at the top of his voice like a madman. (*His mind is now far away*) [. . .] and I would pull the blanket tight, tight over my ears lest I should hear, and I would pray [. . .] pray to be able to sleep and escape from it all [. . .] but she couldn't escape [. . .] she couldn't [. . .][19]

The subsequent section of the Man's memory of the troubled relationship between the mother and father seems to draw directly on Parry's own experience of life during the war. The Man recalls moments of intense inner peace when his mother would come into his room to sleep while the father was away and he would nestle in her lap: 'the wind and rain and him outside and the two of us safe . . . It was good when he was away – just Mam and me.'[20] The notion that this is a direct echo of Parry's own experience is hard to dismiss, as is the idea that this memory is central to the conception of a male identity fluctuating between boyhood, manhood and fatherhood (with the corresponding view of woman as a composite object: mother, temptress and wife).

The other male figure in the play, the Fair Owner, is presented at first as one of great authority and power. Significantly, however, he does not appear in person during Act I, and this creates an opportunity to inflate his reputation and our sense of his effect on those around him. The Boy and Girl from the fair – whose initial impact on the action suggests a grotesque sexuality and violence – are his agents, and carry out his orders almost to the point of murder; but the most obvious symbol or 'insignia' of his power is, of course, the fair. From the very beginning, we see the Man of the House acknowledging its potent influence: his theft of the Dummy is a terrified gesture of defiance against it; and later, as he looks on through his telescope, he is dismayed by the sight of a young couple turning away from the sea to go to amuse themselves in the 'cursed' place. One of the main causes of such a negative connotation for the fair is its reliance on automation. It is a programmed production line of thrills which subjects the individual to a greater, mechanical agency in order to experience pleasure (a fact which contrasts markedly with the Man of the House's desire to make the mechanical, inanimate Dummy into a human through the unfettered exercise of the imagination). However, much as we might wish to empathize with the Man's opposition to the fair, we – as audience to a theatre production – are made to share an awareness of its power. Like the fair, the play itself is also a kind of pre-programmed thrill ride, whose effect of freeing the audience's imagination is counteracted by the fact that it has been primed and rehearsed to do so. It possesses both 'human' and 'mechanical' aspects, and allows us to see the miraculous, expansive transformation of the Dummy into a woman but also the reductive transformation of the Man, and eventually the stage, into a machine.

When the Fair Owner does appear, his reputation has been so precipitated by the Man's anxieties and by the intercession of the fairground 'heavies' that he cannot but strike us as something of a disappointment, an almost comical anticlimax. He is just a man, and a rather gaudily dressed one at that: '*the FAIR OWNER appears at the door. He is a fat man with a hard brown hat on his head, a red waistcoat and a colourful costume, and carries a small whip in his hand.*'[21] His costume is perfectly appropriate of course: he resembles a circus ringmaster, a figure who exerts control over spectacle from afar, rather than one who is intimately implicated in his own fantasies, like the Man of the House. But, as a living, breathing presence, he cannot inspire the same awe and fear in us as he did in the Man, and therefore – regardless of the Man's continuing dissociative terror during Act II – we begin to question, and thus erode, the Fair Owner's authority. And the more he is drawn into the action, the weaker he becomes.

Act II is a transitional phase in the relationship between the Man and the Fair Owner, and plays a vital role in developing our awareness of the underlying narrative of the Man's trauma. But it is tortuously long, and the central device, the conversation between the Man and the Dummy which goes on unbeknown to the Fair Owner, is drastically overplayed. His relationship with the Dummy cannot really develop beyond the point of reverie and rapture which it reached in Act I, and it gradually stagnates here. The crucial moment in the Act comes when the Fair Owner tries to persuade the Man that his indulgence in fantasy is not only rather grotesque (his love object was, after all, a murderess) but futile: she is 'just [. . .] just [. . .] (*He cannot find an appropriate word*) [. . .] a [. . .] thing',[22] a fact which he forcibly demonstrates by beating, drum-like, on her hollow body. Briefly, the Man is intrigued by the Fair Owner's power as he ecstatically foresees and describes the expansion of his fairground right along the beach – from the current 'Golden Acre', which gives the fair its name, to 'two acres, three, four! Five!';[23] but then, as the Fair Owner prepares to wrap the Dummy up in order to return her to the fair, he is spurred into decisive action, and threatens the Fair Owner with his shotgun.[24]

Thus empowered by a phallus of his own, the Man orders the release of the Dummy, and so completes the enactment of the scenarios which he recounted in the previous Act, in which the son fantasizes about being old enough, and brave and powerful enough, to save his mother from the violent attentions of the father. However, rather than merely leading to a resolution of the dramatic situation, the Man's empowerment instigates further change, this time in the theatrical representation of the action. When the Girl from the fair, outside the shack, expresses concern about the Fair Owner, the Man sends her away; but he does so by taking on the Fair Owner's voice. So begins a process of transformation which will come to dominate the rest of the Act, in which the Man not only (literally) outguns the Fair Owner but also comes to embody him in terms of his costume, bearing, voice and accent. Gleefully, he begins to make an automated exhibition of him, by forcing him to dance at riflepoint until '*the roof clatters and the floor shakes*'.[25] Now fully armed against the Fair Owner, the Man claims the identity of the unborn son of the violent father who was responsible for killing the mother's child while it was still in the womb. It was this loss that stole the rose from her cheeks and scraped the gold from her hair, and the Man screams that 'No man ever hated his father the way I hated you!'[26] The Fair Owner vainly tries to persuade him that he is no father to him, but the Man will have none of it, subjecting the Fair Owner to a trial in which he is stripped of his distinctive costume and subjected to a chaotic interrogation somewhat reminiscent of the blackly comic school and trial scenes in *Poen yn y Bol*. The Man and the Dummy bark the charges laid against him in a culminating frenzy:

DUMMY: I accuse you of [. . .]
MAN: Cruelty!
DUMMY: Violence!
MAN: Oppression!
DUMMY: Murder!
MAN: (*shouting loudly*) And erecting a fair![27]

His sentence is to 'cease to exist' by having his identity entirely effaced, and his role usurped by the Man who now, having adopted the Fair Owner's accent, his manner and his costume, forces him to sign over his creation, his phallic insignia. The Fair Owner, in desperation, turns to the Dummy, acknowledging her as a living presence for the first time and pleading for forgiveness. The Man, of course, seizes on this seemingly ridiculous weakness and repeats the Fair Owner's denial of her sentience from the previous act: 'Hey! Are you sane, you crazy devil? (*He points at the Dummy*) She's nothing but [. . .] but a thing!'[28]

In a sense, the logic of the play has been played out by this point. The powerless son has become the potent father, and the father the son. But the action does not end there. Parry adds the final transformation, in which '*using every device possible – sound, lights, moveable flats etc* [. . .] *the House on the Sand turns into a fair*.'[29] It is a move which suggests that he was looking for another *coup* to follow the ringing of the telephone in *Saer Doliau*; and, as before, he tried to use theatre as a means of transcending ordinary reality and giving form to the impossible. The precise effect which he had in mind is not easy to ascertain, but some further context to his intention is offered by the end of the television version of the script, which notes that the director should try to 'convey that the house on the sand fuses <u>with</u>, and finally vanishes <u>into</u> the Fair'.[30] This would be easy enough to accomplish on screen in a series of dissolves; but on stage the fusion recommended above could not be presented in the same way. The synopsis for the English translation in 1977 is similarly vague, but does at least give some idea of the preferred mechanics of the device: 'the whole set at the end of the play revolves so that the House on the Sand becomes part of the fair.'[31] Despite its increased clarity (and the fact that it retains the basic dramaturgical sense of a revolution in action) it remains somewhat unsatisfying because the established relationship between characters and spectators remains unaffected by the final triumph of the phallic fairground. This limitation is transcended in later comments on the play, where Parry proposes that the entire theatre should be implicated in the finale. When outlining a possible operatic version of *Tŷ ar y Tywod*, Parry suggested that the chorus which was to provide accompanying and atmospheric vocals should 'walk through the audience and assemble on the stage to present a song of praise to the fair – then a blackout – the sound of the sea [. . .] Silence'.[32]

It could be that this interpretation of the final scene of *Tŷ ar y Tywod* goes beyond what Parry intended in 1968 and belongs to a later stage in Parry's work, when his treatment of theatrical form was bolder and more inclined towards breaking out of the confines of the stage (this is certainly the case with his staging instructions for the action of later plays such as *Sal* and *Panto*). But it is entirely consistent with the implicit metatheatricality of the material. The very presence of the Dummy as a central device in *Tŷ ar y Tywod*, mirroring and emphasizing the audience's own active/passive engagement with the play, indicates that Parry's practice as a dramatist was already clearly orientated towards the implication of the spectators into the action. As such, the plot of the play is a secondary consideration, and, as with *Saer Doliau*, his main purpose was to create a communication between 'a character on stage and a character in the audience'.[33]

Critical response to *Tŷ ar y Tywod* was somewhat mixed. Huw Ethall, chronicling his week at the National Eisteddfod, described it as '[a]nother star and the ending theatre-perfect'.[34] However, a digest of responses by students from Trinity College Carmarthen published in Theatr Cymru's in-house magazine *Llwyfan* suggests that there was a significant appreciation for the play's theatricality but also a feeling of hostility towards what a number felt was its wilful obscurity.[35] 'J.L.M.', reviewing the television broadcast of the play on 22 December 1968, took advantage of the opportunity to criticize the stage production: 'It has to be said that the version which was televised appeared far more substantial and worth discussing than the stage version, which was more of a theatrical stunt than anything else.'[36] 'Meic' in *Y Cymro* disagreed and succeeded in condemning both the stage and televised versions for inflating material which was appropriate only for a short play, and for giving the lead role to such a deeply unsympathetic character as the the Man of the House.[37] 'J.L.M.'s television review also gives some clues to the changes which Parry made in adapting it for the screen. He praised George P. Owen's production for its filmed inserts and the clarity with which it 'disentangled' the literal representation from the elements of symbolism, particularly in those sequences featuring the Mother, a character who does not, of course, appear in the published stage version. We are given a tantalizing glimpse of Owen's interpretation: 'we saw the ability and imagination of the producer in the undressing scene with the sudden change from the girl to the mother.'[38] The experience of subjecting the play to production and of reviewing the material over the years appears to have convinced Parry of the need to explicate the various manifestations of the Dummy, and to ensure that she operated as only one image of the Man's fluctuating desire rather than a conflated embodiment of it. Parry's later operatic synopsis differentiates between those scenes which feature the Dummy as 'Lisa' and those which present a 'motherfigure'; and he notes quite directly that the 'houseowner's identification with the boy and the association of the fairground owner with the father are figments of his imagination.'[39] It is a sign that, as he matured, he would use theatrical effect in a more discrete and specific way rather than for the kind of cathartic totality which was evident in the first stage version of *Tŷ ar y Tywod*.

5

'A Welsh Tom and Jerry':
Fo a Fe and *Y Ffin*

Internal reorganization of the BBC in 1969 saw the Parrys move
from Caernarfon to Cardiff, with Gwenlyn continuing his work
as a script editor for drama. The move from Caernarfon to Cardiff
was a momentous one for Parry, and he became firmly rooted in
the city for the rest of his life. It was also the year in which he and
Joye had their first daughter, Sian Elin (to be followed two years
later by a second daughter, Catrin Lynwen).

1969 was also, of course a momentous year in Wales, with much
celebration of, and protest against, the investiture of the Prince of
Wales. Gwenlyn's response to these events was firmly hostile: he
had been a Welsh nationalist for a number of years and had already
taken an active part in campaigning for Plaid Cymru's electoral
candidate for Arfon, Dafydd Orwig, in 1959. Such a political profile
was, formally at least, incompatible with his position as a script
editor at the BBC, where employees were required to sign an agree-
ment committing them to desist from overt political bias and to
demonstrate impartiality. It was little wonder, then, that when
accused of serious political bias in 1968 in his work, Parry was
deeply alarmed. He received a letter from the House of Commons
complaining specifically about the series *Byd a Betws*, for which he
was script editor; this serial, it was claimed, was particularly suspect
and was to be investigated, along with other examples of Welsh-
language BBC drama for evidence of political bias. According to the
letter, the public nature of the complaint had led to 'detailed research'
into the allegation by Mr Cledwyn Hughes: 'The conclusion of his
research was that there was a good deal of truth in the charge that

has been made.'[1] Gwenlyn exploded in fury, and was 'supported' in the process of drafting a reply by his colleague Huw Lloyd Edwards: 'He went as far as to help me draft a clever response, my temperature rising with each audacious sentence he suggested.' Of course, at the very last moment before the letter was delivered, Lloyd Edwards confessed all. Having acquired the requisite headed notepaper, he had written the complaint himself, and Gwenlyn had fallen for it: 'he had the ability to take the joke just far enough so that one was bound to realize in the nick of time . . . Then he would laugh until he was sick while I cursed.'[2]

Joke or not, there were others who took Gwenlyn's political affiliations very seriously. Shortly before the investiture ceremony, he received a visit from the police, who informed him that they had noticed a parity between his own whereabouts and certain incidents in the current bombing campaign conducted by *Mudiad Amddiffyn Cymru* [The Movement for the Defence of Wales]. Although this parity was quite coincidental (Parry had been on speaking engagements with various local societies and on work-related trips to Cardiff), the knowledge that his movements were being monitored was alarming. On the day of the investiture itself, his house and movements were very openly watched and followed by a uniformed police motorcyclist.

Such threats did not, however, dissuade Gwenlyn from taking political action where he felt moved to do so. Along with his colleague Meredydd Evans, he defied the BBC's official disapproval by taking an active part in campaigns for *Cymdeithas yr Iaith Gymraeg*, [The Welsh Language Society]; and the two were ironically amused when, having participated in a protest against the dearth of Welsh-language information and leaflets at the Head Post Office on Westgate Street, Cardiff, they discovered that the whole event had been filmed by news cameras from the corporation's commercial rival, TWW.[3] Some years later, he was also involved (along with sixty-six other notables) in the celebrated 'kidnap' of a member of *y Gymdeithas* who was due to appear in court charged with conspiracy to cause criminal damage to the Blaenplwyf television transmitter as part of the campaign for a Welsh fourth television channel. Such causes remained very close to his heart throughout his life.[4] Attacks against them were amongst the very few things that could rouse him to serious anger, according to his colleague John Hefin; a perceived slight or an inherent prejudice against the Welsh language and culture could reduce him almost instantly to an inarticulate rage.

The move to Cardiff saw Parry's work at the BBC develop in earnest. While the Drama department was still resident in Bangor, Parry had created and edited storylines for his first television serial, *Byd a Betws*, which centred on the arrival of a young minister in a seaside village. This was followed by *Y Gwyliwr*, produced in 1970, about a local newspaper in a town much like Aberystwyth; and, following the move to Cardiff, *Tresarn* in 1972, written by the afore-mentioned Huw Lloyd Edwards. There were popular adaptations too, such as *Lleifior*, adapted from Islwyn Ffowc Elis's novels, and the ambitious historical drama series *Yr Ystafell Ddirgel* ['The secret room'] which was an account of Welsh Quakers in America in the eighteenth century, adapted from Marion Eames's historical novel, and which required an eventful research trip to Philadelphia. But, undoubtedly, his most successful BBC project at this point was the co-writing of the sitcom *Fo a Fe* with Rhydderch Jones.

The working relationship between Rhydderch and Gwenlyn had quickly developed after their initial stint as part of the writing team for *Stiwdio B*. They collaborated closely, either as co-writers or as writer and script editor, on a number of productions, some of which were clearly based on their common personal experience, such as National Service (which yielded the co-written television script *Jones 303*) and teaching (which was reflected in Rhydderch's highly successful film *Mr Lollipop MA*, a gentle Ionescoan fantasy about a school lollipop man who, in the privacy of his home, enacts the fantasy of being a teacher). *Fo a Fe* originated from a script written by Rhydderch in 1965, about a young north Walian man who had married a south Walian girl and had gone to live with her 'in a town in South Wales such as Caerphilly'.[5] The BBC showed some interest in this, being particularly keen to try to create a series that would appeal equally to audiences in the north and south of

Wales. Rhydderch's original outline had the older man, Tom Thomas (known as Twm Twm), gently corrupting his son-in-law by taking him into 'all kinds of situations' and thus creating a dilemma for the young wife, who would have to choose to stand up either for her father or her husband. However, the producers, Meredydd Evans and Jack Williams, 'felt that it needed another "tag"', and so the sitcom had not been developed for production. It was this extra component that was provided by Gwenlyn, and, once again, by his observation of his immediate circumstances:

> Gwenlyn's father had retired from working in a quarry in North Wales and had come down to Cardiff to visit him. Being aware of his father's excitement about city life, and thinking about my script, gave Gwenlyn the needed ingredient. The central plot would be based on the conflict between the two fathers-in-law rather than between the young husband and the father-in-law.[6]

This new development gave the basic scenario additional conflict, as the two older men could now create tension not only between the young couple but between each other as well. It also stressed the pervasive presence of Gwenlyn's father in different aspects of his creative process and dramatic characterization: the conflation of his father's experience with his own, and the consequent clash of ideas of maleness, it seemed, were never far from the forefront of his writing. He described the show as a combination of identities: 'it's possible that *Fo a Fe* were Rhydderch and me – it's possible that they were our characters and our fathers' characters'.[7] The relationship between the two old men certainly bore some resemblance at least to that between Parry and Jones: more than a friendship, it resembled a symbiosis, but was marked by often tempestuous bouts of bruising honesty, out of which a deep respect and a joint identity was formed. 'I don't think I could write with anyone else the way I wrote with Rhydderch', Parry noted years later, 'sometimes taking an episode each, sometimes co-writing – and often with no idea who had written what by the end.'[8]

The casting of the show also maintained a number of close personal and professional links, with the extraordinary Ryan Davies memorably taking the lead role as Twm Twm; Guto Roberts (who had been Theatr y Gegin's original choice to take the role of Ifans in *Saer Doliau*) playing the northern father, Ephraim Huws; and Gaynor Morgan Rees – who had already played the Girl in *Saer Doliau* and the Dummy in *Tŷ ar y Tywod* (and would go on to play the Visitor in *Y Ffin*) as Diana the daughter; Clive Roberts completed the cast as George, the northern son.

Partly because of the enormous popularity of Ryan Davies, the show was a hit, and fulfilled its brief of gaining an audience in the north and south. This was no mean feat, given that there was a significant difference in terms of language, character and thus sense of humour between the two parts of Wales. Gwenlyn noted the importance of Ryan's contribution to the balance between the two 'cultures', particularly in view of the fact that his role in the show had been based on the extraordinary Caernarfon character, Wil Napoleon: 'Ryan could turn every northernism which insisted on poking its way into dialogue which should have been southern – he could turn it upside-down.'[9] To the writers' surprise, *Fo a Fe* also appealed to a sizeable non-Welsh speaking audience, too, although that was hardly surprising given Davies's penchant for physical clowning, and the fact that the central comic relationship was archetypal as opposed to being specifically Welsh in its context. Gwenlyn described the two as 'a Welsh Tom and Jerry', but argued that, as with the cartoon series, the success of the partnership lay not in the conflict between them but in the fact that each was comic in his own right.

The close, querulous relationship of the two old men in *Fo a Fe* had already been seen in Parry's drama. It was highly evident in *Tŷ ar y Tywod*, and was also, to a lesser extent perhaps, explored in the clash between the *Saer* and the Lad in *Saer Doliau*. Its next manifestation would be in the relationship between the two main characters in the stage play, *Y Ffin*. The way in which that relationship was portrayed in the stage plays was somewhat different from its representation in Parry's television work, of course; but the element of continuity throughout is undeniable and important. Indeed, there would be a constant interchange between Parry's writing for stage, television and film throughout his life, and although he preferred different media at different times, his preoccupations and inclinations as a writer seem to have remained remarkably consistent throughout. The main difference between his plays for the stage and his works for the screen was that the former were often approached as a kind of 'therapy', while the latter were written 'to order' (no wonder, then, that he habitually referred to Meredydd Evans, head of light entertainment at the BBC, as 'the Colonel'). But Parry was quite content to write to order, or to a given formula: he was anything but precious about writing as a 'worker' rather than as an 'artist' (or, as R. M. Jones put it in a series of questions for interview in 1974, Parry had a 'good deal of respect for hackwork').[10] Another difference was that his writing for television tended to produce work in a lighter vein, a fact which, along with the fundamentally 'disposable' nature of popular television, meant that it was often considered to be of negligible seriousness compared with the stage plays. As he retired from the BBC, he noted that some critics had even 'accused [him] of being 'a literary schizophrenic' because of the difference between his 'serious symbolic' work for the stage and his 'lighter, more natural' pieces for television. Parry himself, however, did not couch the difference between stage and screen in such terms: a continuity of vision between the two was possible, and the fundamental difference was not one of tone but of context in production and reception. Television drama and comedy were very different from stage drama in terms of the environment in which they were shown and the quality of attention paid to both by the audience; and the scheduling of television comedy also made a considerable difference to its reception (scheduling *Fo a Fe* next to news programming, for example, could change its context entirely, making the interpretation of the comedy conspicuously 'close to reality' in a way that theatre was not).[11] Writing for the theatre, though it allowed him to channel and animate images from his unconscious, was nonetheless just as subject to constraint as his work for television. He imposed strict conditions upon himself: to make sure that his plays could be producible within about two and a half hours, so that the audience's capacity to concentrate was not compromised by the fullness of their bladders, and to make sure that they (and the cast) could comfortably get to a pub before closing time. In either case, in the theatre or on television, the cardinal sin was the same: to be boring.

Y Ffin was the final play in what came to be described as Parry's 'trilogy'. It was commissioned by the National Eisteddfod, and first performed by Cwmni Theatr Cymru at Rhuthun in 1973. The definition of the play as the third part of a trilogy seems to have come fairly late; there was no reference to a triad of plays at the time of publication of *Tŷ ar y Tywod* or *Saer Doliau*. Indeed, there is every reason to believe that *Y Ffin* had been planned and mapped out in Parry's mind a number of years previously, even before the writing and production of *Tŷ ar y Tywod*. In his introduction to the published version of *Y Ffin*, John Hefin notes that, sometime after *Saer Doliau*, Gwenlyn had related the dramatic scenario of the play to him during a long car journey, but that, when the Eisteddfod and BBC commission came, he had created *Tŷ ar y Tywod* instead. The designation of *Y Ffin* as the third in a trilogy may have been as much of a discovery to Gwenlyn as to anyone else, and more a matter of opportunistic labelling than design.

However, the fact that he acknowledged a distinct formal relationship between *Y Ffin* and its predecessors gives the play a special status. It makes it the end of a process; the closing of an extended three-play exploration or statement, as if Parry were declaring that his next play would follow a different course and that a previously applied set of guiding presuppositions was now exhausted. It certainly feels like a closing statement: *Y Ffin* is the bleakest of his three full-length works to this date. It lacks even the residual optimism of *Saer Doliau*, and the sparing nature of its staging tends to make the mechanical delights of *Tŷ ar y Tywod* seem rather garish by comparison. But its retrospective designation as the last of a trilogy has a deeper implication: it suggests that Parry was aware of the fact that he had created a play that was based around the same kinds of devices which had been seen in his previous two works, and that he needed to move on. It also suggests a certain disquiet on his part that, after *Saer Doliau* and the success of some of his television work, he was being judged not only according to his own personal concerns and ideas but also according to the public persona of 'Gwenlyn Parry, dramatist'.

Y Ffin ['The border'] (1973)

In the play, an aging middle-aged man, Wilias, leads a young companion, Now, to a ruined shepherd's hovel high up on a mountain. Wilias has led him up to the hovel on the pretext that this is to be their home, but after taking one look at the place, Now is incredulous, and rejects the entire scheme. He goes through the motions of leaving, but eventually chooses to remain rather than return to the unfriendly world below. The two men eventually put the hovel into an acceptable order, but their harmonious relationship is disturbed by the arrival of a temporarily blinded climber who has become lost on the mountain during a snowstorm. This Visitor – another of Parry's mythically disruptive women – remembers nothing of the ordeal that has brought her to this place. The men allow her to stay, but begin to compete for her attention. She, possibly innocently, exacerbates the tension between them by inflating their sense of their self-importance and independence. The jealousy and antipathy between them grows to the point where they draw a line down the middle of the floor of the hovel in order to delineate their own exclusive territory, which only the Visitor may cross. This escalates into a full-scale war between the two, and the construction of a 'border', a barricade, assembled out of the furniture and very walls of the hovel itself. By the time they have completed this, the Visitor has silently departed, leaving them together, alone, bleating 'Miss' after her like lost sheep. The stage lights dim to reveal only their desperate faces before a final blackout.

Parry's own note about the origin of the play described it as a response to 'a lift given to a madman',[12] a fact which suggests strongly that the starting point for the play was the character of Wilias, rather than the erection of the border which gives *Y Ffin* its title. But if this 'madman' was the starting point of the play, we must be somewhat circumspect about his relationship to the character of Wilias. The notion that Wilias is mad, for example, is not to be taken literally (and the term is itself unhelpful): this is not a play that explores, debates or even seeks to reconfigure the notion of insanity. The main purpose of giving Wilias, and Now, a set of characteristics and a past which suggests that they have been subject to a mental breakdown of some sort is to create ambiguity, and to free Wilias in particular from being fully accountable to the audience.

In that respect, it is tantalizing to suggest that he is a self-conscious, and provocatively ironic, reflection of Gwenlyn himself and of his assessment of his reputation as a writer. He shares a number of Parry's characteristics: he is, broadly speaking, a naive fantasist; and, as we have seen, Parry's trilogy had shown him to be preoccupied with notions of dreaming and innocence. It would also be fair to describe Wilias as a frightened manipulator and a fraud, a figure who suggests a highly negative – possibly ironic – projection of Gwenlyn's self-image, and a feeling of alienation from his public persona. Another fascinatingly apposite aspect of Wilias is the fact that he ascribes to himself a religious significance which is well beyond his competence. Within the first few moments of arriving at the hovel, dishevelled in a long coat and plimsolls (the very clothes which the roadside 'madman' is thought to have worn),[13] he removes his scarf and reveals a minister's dog collar underneath. This is a surprise for the audience, and changes our understanding of the context and significance of his actions and the possible history of his life entirely; but, by suddenly skewing the play towards a religious interpretation, it is also a moment that seems all too aware of its audience's expectations of a 'Gwenlyn Parry' play, and it simultaneously satisfies and confounds them by oversupplying the necessary ingredient. This, again, hints at a self-awareness at the heart of Y Ffin which is far more overt than his previous full-length works.

Alongside the fantasist Wilias, and acting as a counterbalance to his capriciousness, is the literally-minded and rather brutishly child-like Now. Now is an ideal foil for Wilias's inventive, rather untrustworthy nature. He is stolid and somewhat credulous, and provides

Wilias with the kind of ready audience which he appreciates. He is also the more physical of the two, and is evidently quite easily roused to passion and to inarticulate – and excessively violent – fury. Together, they form a symbiotic pairing which has distinct echoes of Beckett's duos Estragon and Vladimir, and Hamm and Clov, wherein one partner is intellectually or imaginatively dominant, the other physically. As in Beckett's work, there is a sense in which they constitute a single entity, divided along the Cartesian line which demarcates the mind from the body. However, the relationship between Parry's duo is far more dynamic and engaged than that between Beckett's characters, who know full well that they have exhausted any creative possibilities available to them and are resigned to their incapacity to change their circumstances. Parry's duo are plagued by (false) hope, by the prospect of building a life for themselves which might be free from the interference of 'others' who fail to understand them and thus abusively objectify them, proscribing their freedom. Once again, there is a distinct theatrical dimension to the characters' sense of themselves and of their relationship here, one which (with a certain mischievous irony perhaps) suggests an existence which is assailed and threatened by the prejudices of an unnamed mass.

When they arrive at the designated idyll which Wilias has allegedly bought for them, however, Now is deeply disappointed. It is no more than a skeletal structure surrounded by piles of rubbish. He curses Wilias and decries his useless preoccupation with fantasy, including his religious affiliation, which he criticizes as make-believe and superstition. Ironically, however, when Now himself tries to leave the hovel he does not get far before being forced to return, shamefaced, because of his fear of the dark. In that sense, he, like Wilias, is also subject to the power of fantasy, either positive or negative. Indeed, their relationship is sustained by their capacity to share dreams and images, and they frequently lose themselves in moments of comic play or play-acting. Sometimes, these moments have the effect of denying or deflecting their fears – such as the fear of dying in the hovel, far from civilization, in which case the survivor will be forced to slide down the mountainside at breakneck speed astride a coffin, 'through the heather like a Maserati'.[14] At other times, they are used to galvanize their strength and their sense of togetherness, particularly when aimed against their oppressors, the 'others'. This is seen early in Act I, when Wilias and Now climb up to the loft of the hovel, and confront the audience, who thus become identified as their enemies. This device is particularly interesting for its comic assertion of the audience's mystification at the spectacle, which is possibly another ironic comment by Parry on the reception and interpretation of his work:

> WILIAS: [. . .] we're not going to let some trivialities come between us. Look. (*He stares in the direction of the audience*) [. . .] You see them?
> NOW: Who?
> WILIAS: That lot over there! [. . .] hundreds of them staring at us.
> NOW: (*beginning to take an interest in Wilias's game now*) Hundreds?
> WILIAS: Of all sorts – can't understand what we're doing here, but we won't move for them. (*Raising his voice and confronting his imaginary audience*) WE WON'T MOVE FOR YOU![15]

At other times, the interplay is genuinely symbiotic, and signals a return to the rather overripe naivety which characterized the Man of the House's relationship with the Dummy in *Tŷ ar y Tywod*. Once they have rebuilt the hovel, Wilias surprises Now by revealing that he has put the deeds to it in both their names. Now is touched by this revelation, and weeps; and the scene is then given over to an extended and elaborate series of fantasy scenarios in which they firstly dream about their impending life of self-sufficient, honest toil, and then dance together, playfully exchanging romantic platitudes:

> NOW: (*smiling as he has an idea for another game*) May I have the pleasure of this dance, sir?
> WILIAS: (*bowing*) Of course, madam. (*The two of them begin to dance around the room*)
> NOW: Do you come here often?
> WILIAS: I'll come here more often now, having met you.[16]

As in *Tŷ ar y Tywod*, Parry plays with a sense of affection unbounded, but one which advertises its naivety by ignoring the distinction between adult sexuality and childish play. After their pseudo-romantic dance, they fall to the floor, with Now falling on top of Wilias, tickling him. The homoerotic connotations of these frolics are hard to ignore, and there is a distinct sense of provocative mischief about Parry's faux-innocence. But the denying of any sexual significance to Now and Wilias's childlike behaviour, the assertion that their play knows nothing of the sexual nature of being, serves a distinct narrative purpose. It makes them 'golden age' incorruptibles, and their hovel a proto-Eden; all the better to emphasize the fall from grace which will imminently follow, and the negative symbiosis of competitiveness and violence.

The pair are disturbed by the arrival of an 'other', in the form of an injured and temporarily-blinded climber who has become lost on the mountain during the snowstorm which now rages outside. She is another – the last – of Parry's siren women, and has a number of the doll-like characteristics of her predecessors: she is lost in the men's world on the mountain, she is blind and reliant on their charity, and she has no memory of the ordeal which has brought her to this place. Like the Dummy in *Tŷ ar y Tywod*, she is a fantasy object whose devotion is craved but who becomes largely forgotten once the power struggle between the two men (which she has helped to instigate) escalates into violence; and, importantly, like the Girl in *Saer Doliau*, her function is to undermine or usurp the authority of the main character. She does this not only by appealing to the implicit vanity of Wilias's imagination, coquettishly praising him for his mature worldly-wisdom, but also by taking over his role as a manipulator of audience expectation. Throughout Act I, the action of the play was allowed to develop according to the gradual revelation of Wilias's personal circumstances and his motivation for seeking out the hovel. The audience were in thrall to his power: for example, what was interpreted as his ecstatic arrival at the hovel soon had to be re-evaluated as a *return* to it, after he revealed to Now (and to the audience) that he himself was the previous inhabitant. But once the Visitor arrives, it is she whose identity is unknown and who provides the surprises: Wilias finds himself as ignorant of the truth of her situation as we are.

This manipulative reversal is given very direct and effective expression. Wilias tries to help the Visitor to remember, but most facts about her previous existence evade her. She is more engaged with a sensory response to her surroundings, and asks if she might be allowed to try to 'see' him by touching his face with the tips of her fingers. He consents, but is placed in a position of unfamiliar and distinctly uncomfortable passivity as a consequence. Moreover, unlike Now and the audience, she has not been taken in by Wilias's attempts to project an image of himself as a Man of God through his costuming; and, once she touches his dog collar and loudly declares that he is a minister, Wilias urges her to be quiet. The direct and intimate nature of her contact with him seems to shame him into a denial of that identity which, on a visual level, he has tried to assert from the beginning of the play.

The gradual deterioration in the relationship between the two men ensues, as they compete with each other for the attentions and affections of the Visitor. This has the effect of objectifying all concerned, with the Visitor being defined as a mere prize in the battle between the two men, and the men themselves reduced to ever more juvenile patter in their defence of their territory. The difference between these two parallel kinds of objectification is interesting: the Visitor remains largely unchanged in terms of her nature and status, as her identity as an object (and as a symptom of Parry's response to what he described as the 'mystery' of femininity) has already been established; but the reductive 'objectification' of the men is comically grotesque, and constitutes the deterioration of a dual (symbiotic) subject. They become ever more childish in their speech and rhetoric as their competition for the Visitor's attention and affection intensifies:

NOW: Well, it's high time breakfast got made isn't it?
WILIAS: (*Exchanging the soup bowl for another*) And you know that I was supposed to make it today.
NOW: You made it yesterday!
WILIAS: You did!
NOW: You did!
WILIAS: And you let the milk boil over the stove.

NOW: That was the day before.
WILIAS: Yesterday!
NOW: The day before.
WILIAS: Yesterday![17]

This fall from the grace of brotherly affection accelerates as the two take up rudimentary weapons against each other, each befitting the wielder's personality (Now brandishes a shovel, Wilias a bread-knife), and then create the borderline which gives the play its title. At first, this is constituted as a simple line down the middle of the room, then as a curtain and finally as a full scale barricade, using every piece of timber available – even the walls of the hovel itself. Their separation only emphasizes their fixation with each other, and with each other's potential duplicity, which is alleviated only by the promise of the Visitor's approval. However, once the barricade is erected, and the hovel ruined, she departs unnoticed, leaving the two of them alone. Their degeneration is completed as the lights are dimmed around them and we lose sight of the stage, even the barrier that they built:

WILIAS: Miss [. . .] can you hear me [. . .]?
(*Their voices are now just like two children crying for their mother.*)
NOW: Say something [. . .]
WILIAS: He's no good to you [. . .]
NOW: What would you do with an old man like that?
(*Their speech slows down as if they were under the influence of drugs.*)
WILIAS: You can't trust him – he's dangerous [. . .]
NOW: But [. . .] but I'm ready to wait [. . .] I'm ready to wait until you're ready.
WILIAS: I'll wait [. . .] I'll wait until you come [. . .]
(*Silence. By now the stage should be completely dark except for the two faces either side of the barrier.*)
NOW: Miss [. . .] (*Almost like the bleat of sheep.*)
WILIAS: Miss [. . .] (*Similarly heartbroken.*)
NOW: Miss (*Darkness – Now's face disappears.*)
WILIAS: Miss (*Darkness – Wilias's face disappears.*)
(*In the darkness we hear the gentle moaning of the wind.*)[18]

Their descent is compelling and horrific, all the more so for showing how the subject's desire for its fantasy object may persist the
level at which discursive speech is destroyed, and at which the
human equates to an abandoned animal. It is a memorably appall-
ing image of self-consciousness extinguished. Now and Wilias are
still alive, of course, and the scene shows not their death but the total
suppression of their ability to express themselves as individuals.
Even as 'sheep', however – beneath the level of language – they
are still fundamentally motivated by a human desire for the object
of their fantasy, even if they can do nothing more now than stupidly
call out her name.

The indignity and suddenness of the men's collapse, along with
the fact that it is bidden merely by the creation of a barrier in a
shepherd's hovel, does have an air of Absurdist black comedy about
it, a fact that is entirely appropriate in a play which seems to borrow
freely from the work of Samuel Beckett. It is not difficult to see that
a number of the scenes already discussed (such as the implicit
addressing of the audience from the loft) point directly to devices
from Beckett's plays, particularly *Endgame*. However, Parry's *homage*
to Beckettian theatricality does as much to point up the important
differences between the two as to emphasize the similarities. In
Beckett, the mockery of meaning is intensely cruel (all the more so
for the concentrated poetry of the characters' speech) and leads to
the evacuation of all expectation. All is reduced, including the
nature and status of the theatrical presentation itself, which is often
implicitly decried by the characters for its monotony, and portrayed
as a kind of inept Vaudeville (or as 'the Book of Job . . . performed
by clowns', in Jan Kott's memorable description).[19] Parry, however,
cannot bring himself to undermine the dignity of theatrical presentation to anything like the same extent: for all its dilapidation, there
is something rather earnest – haunting and potentially tragic – about
the skeletal structure and windswept decay of the shepherd's hovel.
Similarly, Wilias's determination that he and Now may be able to
create a refuge for themselves in this place imbues the action with
a real sense of hope and with an implicit faith in higher meaning.
Parry teases us into entertaining the possibility that the men's

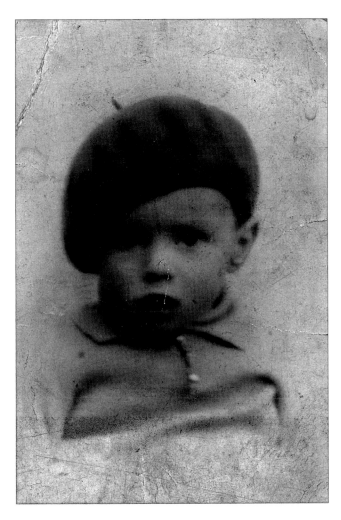

1. Gwenlyn as a child, with his favourite beret, 1930s.

2. Gwenlyn as a teenager, sporting his
St John's Ambulance hat.

3. The Parry family reunited after the war.

4. Brynrefail school football team, 1950. Gwenlyn is in the front row, left.

5. Gwenlyn following his call-up to the RAF, 1950.

6. Gwenlyn with Joye at the Newborough Arms,
Caernarfon, in the early 1960s.

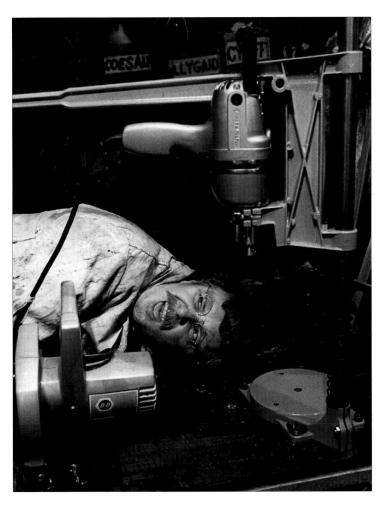

7. Publicity still for Cwmni Theatr Cymru's production of *Saer Doliau*, 1966. David Lyn as the *Saer* is menaced by the newly installed machinery.

8. Gwenlyn engaged in political action, late 1960s. The photograph was mocked up by his friends Ifan Parry and Huw Lloyd Edwards.

9. At home with daughters Sian and Catrin, early 1970s.

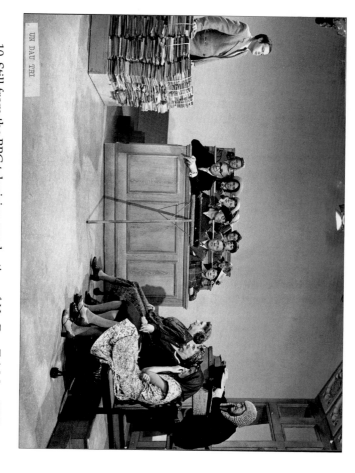

10. Still from the BBC television production of *Un Dau Tri*, May 1972. Clive Roberts as Bili Puw on trial as a 'Conshi'.

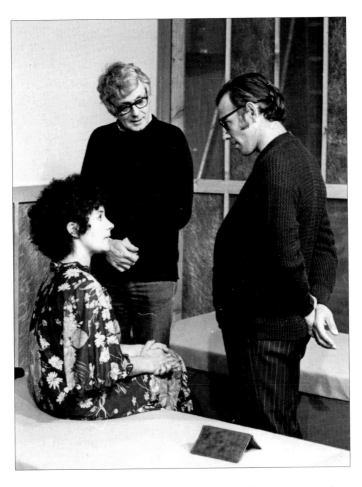

11. Rehearsal for Cwmni Theatr Cymru's production of
Y Tŵr, 1978. David Lyn (centre, background) directing
Maureen Rhys and John Ogwen.

12. Hard at work with his great friend Rhydderch Jones, late 1970s.

13. Siwan Jones in the title role of Cwmni Theatr Cymru's production of *Sal*, 1980.

14. Cwmni Theatr Cymru's controversial production of *Tŷ ar y Tywod*, 1983. The Man of the House (Geraint Lewis) dances, while the 'Passion-Dummy' (Nia Caron) and the 'Mother-Dummy' (Rhian Morgan) look on.

15. Gwenlyn and Ann's wedding day, 1986.

16. On holiday with children Marged and Gruffydd, 1990.

relationship might indicate a kind of transcendence: 'we understand each other you see [. . .] there's nobody else [. . .] we're lucky to have each other [. . .] God arranged for us to meet, you see'.[20] This is quite unlike Beckett: there, the characters are fully aware of the pitifulness of their situation, and have become indifferent of it. Delusions of value have no place in his drama, and when Hamm, Clov and Nagg resort to prayer in *Endgame*, the very thought of 'meaning something' is ridiculed: 'The bastard! He doesn't exist!'[21]

There are some aspects of Parry's dramaturgy, however, which indicate a real mastery of his craft; and, though they may have their origin in Beckett's theatre practice, they are made to serve Parry's ends in full. One of the most important is the lyrical interplay, the kind of duet, which we experience between absence and presence in *Y Ffin*; between light and darkness, sound and silence. The two men encase themselves in their hovel, but in doing so, create a space with a very firmly delineated centre and undelineated edges. These margins of the stage exert an influence on the characters and the audience alike: Now recoils from them when he tries to leave, and is forced back into the middle by fear of what may lurk in their shadows; and the pair's fear of the 'others' is implicitly associated with the darkness at the edge of the stage. This is very closely related to Beckett's consistent use of a black 'nothingness' as a major scenic element in his later work. Beckett also applies the same exchange between 'somethingness' and 'nothingness' in his characters' dialogue: they talk, but such is the indeterminacy of time in plays such as *Waiting for Godot* and *Endgame* that their dialogue is almost perfectly inconsequential. The dramatic situation changes very little as a result of the dialogue; and its effect is really felt in theatrical terms, as it 'wastes' performance time and prolongs the action to the point of despair. But this is where Parry deviates most clearly from Beckett's example: throughout his trilogy, he resists such a daringly theatrical prolongation of time. His dialogue urges his characters, as it were, to 'get on with it'. *Y Ffin* is thus far more traditional in its attempt to define, reveal and resolve the action on stage through dialogue; and so the implied nothingness in the space is offset by the dramaturgical development of the characters' relationship with each other and with the audience. It all tries to amount to something, whereas Beckett is content to let his work – with astonishing poetic force – amount to nothing. Parry could not allow the same thing to happen on his stage because of the implications of such extreme passivity for the language which he loved and which, by means of his artistic efforts, he wished to help sustain.

Cwmni Theatr Cymru's production of *Y Ffin* was directed by John Hefin, and reunited some Gwenlynian stalwarts in the cast: David Lyn as the aging Wilias (he, of course, had previously played Ifans in *Saer Doliau*) and Gaynor Morgan Rees as the Visitor (following her appearance as the Girl in *Saer Doliau* and the Dummy in the stage version of *Tŷ ar y Tywod*). Indeed, the play had been written with these actors in mind. It also featured the young and highly rated Eilian Wyn as Wilias's youthful companion, Now. This was John Hefin's only venture into professional theatre, but not his first experience of working on one of Gwenlyn's stage plays: he had previously directed a lively studio version of *Poen yn y Bol* for the BBC in 1972, under its original title *Un, Dau, Tri*. Once again, the production of Gwenlyn's new play involved the creation of a stage and a television version, and so the appointment of Hefin to direct both ensured a good deal of continuity between the productions. However, by his own admission, Hefin as a director was primarily engaged with the visual aspects of production, and had a mind to allow the eye to do as much of the interpretation as possible, while Gwenlyn thought of *Y Ffin* as primarily a stage play which 'could perhaps lend itself well to television, but not give [itself] to television'.[22]

Critical response to the production was generally favourable, but showed that the designation of Parry's work as a discussion of religion was still very much to the fore. Arthur Morris Jones, responding to the way in which Wilias had placed a cross-like piece of timber between him and Now during the erection of the barricade – a feature which had conspicuously caught the last of the light during the final fade to black – argued that *Y Ffin* was again a religious play, although he noted that 'there would probably be some dispute and argument about this.'[23] Similarly, Gwilym R. Jones argued, almost in spite of himself, for a religious interpretation of the play's imagery: 'I heard one friend giving a religious interpretation of the play. The limp Church is represented by [Wilias], the middle-aged preacher; Now, the young lad, is the advocate of humanism, the humanist optimism which gripped the Church, and the young girl climber who has lost her identity is the secular, materialistic society.' The central boundary itself was indicative of 'the border line which is spreading between believers and non-believers.' However, Jones prefaced his comments with a caveat which suggested that he, and others, were increasingly willing to allow the play to stand on its own merits rather than as a pretext for symbolism: 'Gwenlyn Parry was not aiming to convey any message other than the message which is conveyed by any good play, giving us a theatrical experience which is valuable in itself . . . We get this sincere dramatic pleasure without having to bother very much about what the dramatist is trying to say about life through *Y Ffin*.'[24] And this view was echoed by Charles Huws, reviewing the television broadcast of the play, which (finally) went out in March 1975:

> I remember Gwenlyn Parry driving me mad on a discussion programme soon after [*Saer Doliau*] by refusing to say definitively what was the message of his play. Was the *Giaffar* God or not? Since then there has been much discussion and speculation by literary critics asserting what the dramatist was really trying to say, but 'everything to everyone' and 'you see what you want to see in it' was what Gwenlyn insisted on, and by now I'm willing to accept that as the plain truth. Does a man writing a play have to 'say' anything at all?[25]

6
'In the middle of the seventies experience': *Pobol y Cwm* and *Grand Slam*

The end of *Y Ffin* marked the end of 'the trilogy'. As a series of plays, it had cemented Parry's reputation as an innovative drama-tist, one whose awareness of dramatic form and theatricality had broken new ground, and whose capacity to create a fluent modernist idiom for the Welsh stage had been hugely important in defining a new kind of relationship between the theatre and its audience. He had, almost single-handedly, dragged that audience out of its broad allegiance to amateurism and into the post-war theatre. The trilogy was not without its critics, of course, and those fell broadly into two categories: those who regarded Parry's writing as highly and rather glibly derivative on the one hand, and those who resisted the implicit ambiguity of his vision, seeing it as a proto-nihilistic approval of meaninglessness. R. M. Jones, in particular – writing in 1975, in a critical but also comparatively conciliatory vein – argued that whereas Gwenlyn was certainly asking all the questions, he was offering no answers. Comparing him with another great allegorist, he noted that John Bunyan would have been pretty certain of the meaning of his allegories and the way in which he wanted them interpreted; Parry, on the other hand, was uncertain, and 'this uncertainty, this ambiguity, [was] an intrinsic part of the "meaning" of his plays.'[1]

In many ways, R. M. Jones is right. The plays do present them-selves as allegories, with an implied allusion being made in the action to other, often broader and more encompassing, narratives: *Y Ffin*, for example, consciously plays on the story of the Garden of Eden at several points in its action. But they do not aim to produce a single message or a uniform interpretation, and as such they reveal and enact a fundamental conflict between two sets of cultural values: those which emphasize the power of and need for *collectivity*, and those which emphasize the advantages of *individualism*. As we have seen, this conflict was central to Gwenlyn's assessment of his position in the world: he had been formed in the shadow of some extraordinarily potent collective forces – the Wesleyan Methodism of his chapelgoing youth, the traditional solidarity of the quarrying industry; and, latterly, Nationalism. But, as he had moved from Deiniolen to London, and thence to Caernarfon and Cardiff, these forces – especially the first two – had been revealed to him as particular and contingent, and he had had to re-evaluate his most fundamental beliefs. In John A. T. Robinson's *Honest to God*, he had found an impressive but temporary means by which to redefine his sense of faith: but the plays of the trilogy strongly suggest that, as he matured as a writer, the power of individualism exerted an ever-greater influence upon him such that the last play, *Y Ffin*, indicates the obliteration of collective effort as a means of sustaining a sense of conviction. As Dewi Z. Phillips argues, Gwenlyn's plays reflect the condition of an intelligence gradually drifting away from religious faith and towards a fully secular liberalism.

But the trilogy was completed, and Parry was now committed to something different. If a change of dramatic voice occurred, then it was at least partly prompted by personal circumstances as well as professional ones. William John Parry died early in 1974, following a short hospital stay. It was, of course, a loss that hit Gwenlyn very hard; but as a writer, too, it was the loss of a pivotal figure, the one who, 'with his fantastical tall tales . . . had given him the urge to write' in the first place, and whose influence on Parry's sense of masculinity had been formative.[2] The loss of his father may well have given him an increased sense of his own mortality, too; but he had long been preoccupied with mortality and with the possibility of a life after. Those closest to him knew him to be an extremely super-stitious person, with what he called a 'nose' or sixth sense for myster-ious phenomena. For example, while on holiday in Italy during the late 1960s, he visited Monte Cassino, where his father had been involved in fierce fighting during the liberation of Italy; while there, he felt a strange chill go through him, only to be told upon his return that his father had been injured in a fall at the quarry on the very day when he visited the site of the battle. Gwenlyn had taken this as a sign that his father had somehow involuntarily communicated with him; and so, some years before his father's death, he had asked him to come back and make contact with him after his demise, in order for him to know that there was some form of life hereafter and that there could be some form of connection between worlds. Similarly, after his father's death, and through his BBC colleague Jeffrey Iverson, he had become fascinated by the work of Arnall Bloxham, who had famously been involved in regression hypnotherapy and had helped a number of his subjects to 'recall' several alleged past lives. There was something beyond common knowledge in these stories which appealed greatly to him, and he also claimed to have a deep-rooted memory of a past life of his own.

In the more everyday world of work at the BBC, he had been engaged throughout 1974 on preparations for the launching of the Drama Department's latest Welsh-language television serial. The corporation was unveiling two serials simultaneously: an English-language production set in a Valleys cafe, and a Welsh-language serial set in the semi-industrial south-west. Whereas the English serial (called *Dai Macaroni*) would be soon forgotten, its Welsh-language counterpart, *Pobol y Cwm*, was a huge success, and became a cornerstone of Welsh-language television.

In the first instance, *Pobol y Cwm* 'was Owen Edwards's baby', as Gwenlyn noted in 1988, referring to the head of programmes and controller of BBC Wales at that time. But it was Parry and producer John Hefin who shaped the serial and gave it its distinctive identity. The location for the series – between Llanelli and Carmarthen, broadly in the Gwendraeth valley – was to be a crucial factor, and it was an area which Gwenlyn knew very well. It was in, or at least very close to, Joye's native square mile; and it was also the very same kind of rural-cum-industrial area in which Gwenlyn himself had grown up.

The model for such a serial had, of course, been firmly established by Granada's *Coronation Street*, and *Pobol y Cwm* was bound to follow the same kind of principle of 'fascinating freemasonry', of entertaining 'by examining a community . . . and initiating the viewer into the ways of the people who live there', as Tony Warren, the creator of the *Street*, had written in 1960. Accordingly, Parry and John Hefin were determined to '[d]evelop a storyline full of events which were inconsequential in some respects but which created a believable overall impression of Welsh village life'.[3] To do so, they would have to appeal to a very wide audience, in spite of significant differences in the audience's demographics and its opinion about the cultural and political function of Welsh television. Gwenlyn argued that, as with *Fo a Fe*, the creation of good lightweight material for television ('wallpaper', as he called it)[4] served a seriously important purpose in terms of the viability of the language: without a well-made soap opera, he argued, the popularity of Welsh television would be compromised, and any hope of retaining a broad population with enough Welsh to understand more linguistically demanding stage plays would be effectively killed off. Moreover, he approvingly quoted Dafydd Glyn Jones's general aphorism (after Leslie A. Fiedler) that there were too many 'bad good things' in the world of Welsh literature, and not enough 'good bad things'.[5]

Pobol y Cwm would have to achieve serious ends without showing an immediately serious face, and its guiding principle had to be *hwyl*. John Hefin had decreed that the show, without undermining the credibility of the characters, was to be 'at least 75% humour'. In addition, in spite of the programme's undoubted political significance as a mass-medium portrayal of contemporary society in Welsh, there was to be 'no preaching on the state of the language', nor any other form of overt debating of contemporary issues, 'the evils of drugs, the dangers of sex, theological dogma or anything else'. And, perhaps contrary to the desires of a group such as Adfer, whose policy advocated a return to rural areas of *Y Fro Gymraeg* in order to shore up the language, the show chose characters with names 'like Reg and Wayne rather than Rhodri and Peredur.

Representing the reality of life in the anthracite coalfield was vital if we wanted to attract viewers.'[6]

A team of writers was assembled, which was comprised in the first instance not of experienced television writers but of novelists and stage dramatists: Meic Povey, who acted as Parry's assistant script editor, Marion Eames, Harri Pritchard Jones, Tom Richards, Gwynne D. Evans and Eic Davies (who had been the adjudicator for the Eisteddfod competition in 1961 when Gwenlyn had submitted *Y Ddraenen Fach*). They would provide the dialogue for the scenarios which had already been worked out by the editorial team, although Parry and Povey would both write occasional episodes themselves. It was a huge undertaking, but, alongside everything else, Parry saw to it that the writing team expanded considerably during the following years. He had a deliberate and distinct mission to try to build up the scripting and editing teams for Welsh drama with people he trusted and who were of a like mind.

Pobol y Cwm was first broadcast on 13 October 1974. Its first episode was notable for the rather ingenious gimmick used in order to introduce the characters quickly to the audience. Brynawelon, the old people's home in the series, was visited by the broadcaster Alun Williams, who hosted a popular local meet-the-people show called *Dewch am Dro*, during which the underlying conflicts between the various characters were outlined. It set a pattern by which celebrities would visit the village (such as Max Boyce, the night before a rugby international in March 1975) and interact with the residents: the whole exercise was geared towards attracting public attention and creating a sense of popular momentum. And it worked. In terms of the audience for Welsh-language television at the time, *Pobol y Cwm* became a huge success: by the time of the second series, the characters' lives had become well established topics of conversation, and meetings of local societies were being moved away from Wednesday nights in order to allow members to stay home and watch. But the show's truth to daily life also proved rather too robust for some viewers: the series drew complaints in its early days for the frequency of scenes located in the village pub, the Deri Arms, and also for the implicit approval which this gave to the depiction of the drinking of alcohol. This kind of criticism was indicative of the difference between the various audience constituencies for the show (which happened to correspond closely to David Jenkins's division of Welsh rural societies into *'Buchedd A'* – the people of the chapel – and *'Buchedd B'* – the people of the tavern);[7] and striking a balance between the two was a constant challenge. There were other significant divisions, too: the older generation among the cast had learnt their craft (with one or two honourable exceptions, such as Rachel Thomas) on the amateur stage, and had retained the more direct, rhetorical manner which had been associated with it; the younger actors, meanwhile, had been introduced to television much earlier in their careers and were thus able to adapt their acting style to the needs of the camera. This, according to the television critic Charles Huws, meant that the scenes in the old people's home were somewhat turgid and affected, while those featuring the younger actors – in scenes in the Deri Arms, for example – were far more natural.[8]

But the major point of division occurred around the use of language. Quite soon during the production process, it became clear that *Pobol y Cwm* was attracting a sizeable audience whose Welsh was less fluent, or had little or no Welsh at all (for example, Gwenlyn noted a letter from one viewer asking the cast to speak more slowly in order to ensure her that she had understood everything). The Gwendraeth valley itself – along with many other rural areas – was also becoming increasingly anglicized, and so the attempt to be true to contemporary life brought with it a good many tensions. The way in which *Pobol y Cwm* reflected the profile and use of the language back to its audience was always a matter of discussion and dispute – indeed, that in itself could be said to be one of the serial's most valuable contributions. But there were strict, and rather unrealistic, limits to what it could achieve, a fact which became evident following the highly negative reaction to the introduction of a monoglot English character as the manager of Brynawelon. It was soon realized that the programme, however authentic it wished to be, had to play up the increasingly fantastical notion of a society which had little habitual contact with English and could create its own identity and its own internal authority through its use of the Welsh language alone.

The idea of a self-sustaining fantasy with its own linguistic trajectory, at odds in many ways with daily reality, is a pretty plausible description of Hefin and Parry's other great project of this period, the television film *Grand Slam*. It was yet another example of the way in which Gwenlyn was more than ready to adapt, even – in this case – to abandon, his work to the need for *hwyl*. It was also a project which, during its commissioning, writing, casting and filming, tested the dynamism and value of the relationship between the writer and director to the utmost.

Very generally, the film centres on the story of a father and son, Caradog and Glyn Lloyd-Evans, who go to Paris on a rugby trip to watch Wales play France at the Parc des Princes. For Caradog, the dour village undertaker, the purpose of the journey is not so much to watch the match but to attempt to try to find his lost love, his 'little Butterfly', whom he met and lost during the Liberation of Paris in 1944. He succeeds, but is disillusioned; his son, meanwhile, indulges in a night and day of passion with the woman's daughter, Odette. Such is the plot: but *Grand Slam* is hardly a plot-driven film. Its success and appeal lies in its creation of a narrative form appropriate to the random, hedonistic nature of a rugby trip. It is, in that respect, a very loose and very late Welsh take (or skit) on the French 'new wave' cinema of the 1960s; and, as such, the production process of the film was entirely in keeping with the revolutionary approach of the *nouvelle vague*. It took much pleasure in ruffling feathers within the middle-management bureaucracy of the BBC, capitalizing on Hefin and Parry's recent record of popular successes in situation comedy and drama to bend or suspend conventional rules and practices, and stretch its (insubstantial) budget: with the invaluable backing of the head of programmes in Wales, Geraint Stanley Jones, Hefin threw out the usual procedures and, rather than producing the film on the basis of a complete script and detailed shooting schedules, created the detail of many scenes through actor improvisation. Parry was complicit in this decision, and had to adjust his contribution as screenwriter according to the whims of the cast and the (somewhat random) circumstances of filming on location.

The film had originally been intended as a story, to be produced in Welsh, which followed the Deiniolen Silver Band on a trip to Brussels; but the assistant head of programmes, the veteran television producer D. J. Thomas, rejected this proposal, suggesting instead that it should be based around a rugby trip. Brussels having thus also been discounted, the story became centred on Paris (which was retained even when budgetary constraints led to a strong case being made for Twickenham instead). The cast of characters which Gwenlyn had proposed also changed, for various reasons. In a draft outline of the story in 1975, there are three main characters, the rough and ready Prysor (who would develop, largely untouched, into Mog Jones, played by Windsor Davies), the lothario Gwyn (identified initially as a 'Max Boyce type',[9] but who became the undertaker's son, Glyn, played by Dewi Morris) and the drunken northerner Elis. This last character, identified by Gwenlyn as a '<u>younger</u> Hugh Griffith type',[10] underwent the most complex transformation. He was described as having little interest in the rugby, a characteristic retained in the film by Caradog Lloyd-Evans (the aged undertaker, played by Hugh Griffith himself); his drunkenness became the prime feature of the minor character Wil Posh (played by Dillwyn Owen, most of whose feature scenes had to be cut), and his naive northernness applied to a new character, Trefor. But his place in the scenario was usurped by Maldwyn Novello-Pughe (played by Sion Probert), who was introduced after John Hefin had struck up a friendship with the actor during the filming of the English-language version of Rhydderch Jones's *Mr Lollipop MA*. It was his character who made the most of the opportunity to improvise, and, by Gwenlyn's own admission, there were more of Probert's lines in the final version than his own.

The idea that this film was 'written' by Gwenlyn has to be taken with a fairly large pinch of salt, then, as must the credit given to Gwynne D. Evans as translator (indeed, the idea that the script had been translated was part of an exercise in internal propaganda, so that higher echelons of the BBC would have to acknowledge that work was going on through the medium of Welsh which was innovative and of sufficiently broad appeal to be significant in its own right). Some of the scenes were more thoroughly scripted than others, but many, particularly those involving greater numbers of (male) characters were largely ad libbed. Gwenlyn's role as screenwriter became a matter of trying to keep up with the changes occurring in the rehearsal room and on location and helping the general sense of bonhomie upon which much of the action was reliant. A fine balance had to be achieved between the happily unstructured feel of the characters' adventure in Paris and the structuring of a coherent and appropriate narrative arc, all in limited time and without formally sanctioned access to the stadium and city streets. But it would not have been possible at all without an extremely thorough – almost excessive – attention to detail. Gwenlyn was present throughout the preparation and rehearsal process, and was primed to respond to the vagaries of the process. As he noted in an interview: 'It wasn't just going and doing the film with ha-ha and all the rugby jokes; it had to be real'.[11] His role, in effect, was to create a structured, and occasionally improvised on-the-spot, script edit; and this was nowhere more apparent than in the film's final scene, which was meant to have featured reaction to Wales's victory over France, and their consequent achievement of the Five Nations' Grand Slam. However, Wales lost the match; and there had to be a lightning-quick accommodation of the more downbeat mood during the crew's remaining hours in the city.

The 'authorship' of the film, then, was widely distributed among the participants: the director, the cast, Gwenlyn himself, and – crucially – the man over to whom the whole affair was turned at the end of shooting, the editor Chris Lawrence. For all that, *Grand Slam* was, according to John Hefin, much to Gwenlyn's liking. It brought him into the circle of attention of those who were 'in the middle of the seventies experience', people for whom *Fo a Fe* or *Pobol y Cwm* may have meant nothing. For Gwenlyn, it was confirmation that a loose narrative structure, coupled with a team bonded around the pursuit of *hwyl*, could produce highly popular and successful work, albeit of the 'wallpaper' variety. In that sense, it was a replaying, on a considerably larger scale, of the ludic prank play *La Fontaine*; and an affirmation that success in writing for performance involved both asserting and relinquishing control.

7

'They will also argue and fight and talk about their fear of death etc.': *Y Tŵr*

The success of Parry's trilogy and his television work had secured his career, and had created an enviable reputation for him among Welsh dramatists. Since 1969, he had built a coterie of writers, producers, performers and technical staff around him at the BBC; and now, as a professional Welsh Cardiffian of the 1970s, he – in his own rather idiosyncratic way – cut a bit of a dash. As he eased in to middle age, and especially after the popular success of his television work, he became increasingly theatrical, if somewhat jumbled, in his apparel and appearance, in a leather coat and his trademark Zapata-like moustache, and even – a few years later – a monocle. He was no longer the writer, nor the kind of man, he had been back in the mid-1960s: and the timorousness which he had shown in refusing to stand to acknowledge the audience for *Saer Doliau* was largely a thing of the past.

He had moved on; and the death of his father, as well as his own arrival at the 'end of the beginning' of life, caused other, deeper aspects of his work and personality to change. He was increasingly aware of the way in which he had been, and was being, shaped by time – by events, creative projects, comradeships and losses. As he neared his half-century, he could, rather like the poet Gwenallt, see with ever greater clarity what he had made of himself, and he challenged himself to consider what that achievement meant. His first three plays had all been based in a rather wilfully naive view of the world, in which a fundamentally innocent figure pursued a reintegration of their sense of themselves either through faith or fantasy, and was fatally corrupted in the process. With his next play,

Y Twr, he began the serious business of facing and describing life not as a matter of fantasy, but as the unalterable and accumulated product of existence: as biography. This biographical element had been variously suppressed, denied or confused in the previous plays, but here it was given undeniable prominence. 'Life' was the sum total of an individual's achievements, pressed into a narrative mould rather brutally corresponding to a beginning, a middle and an end. In order to give it theatrical form, however, he would have to change something quite significant about his dramatic technique. Instead of creating a metaphor or an edifice which addressed a sense of one's *place* in the world – as he had done in his previous full-length plays – he would now have to create a work which was fundamentally concerned with *time*. This he did: and, though his Tower does have distinct spatial characteristics, its most salient feature is the way in which it compresses time, and brings that finite and progressional – biographical – idea of life into conflict with the essential sense of infinite possibility, and of eternity, resident in the immediate (theatrical) present.

Y Twr ['The tower'] (1978)

Apart from the death of his own father, *Y Twr* was also inspired by the death of his father-in-law, Roy Davies, to whom the play is jointly dedicated; and by the death of another friend and colleague, the artist Victor Neep, one of whose paintings originally inspired the idea of the Tower. There were also two other important influences on the genesis of the play. The first was a memory of the large staircase of the George Hostel at the Normal College, Bangor, where the students would habitually sit and sing together of an evening. The way in which it wound itself away above their heads offset the sense of the group's togetherness and provided Gwenlyn with rather a haunting image of a generation beginning an upward journey through time, to an unknowable destination.[1] The other influence was the production by Cwmni Theatr Cymru in 1974 of E. A. Whitehead's play *Alpha Beta*, performed as a duet by the actors John Ogwen and Maureen Rhys (Ogwen also translated the play). This play portrays the deteriorating relationship between an unnamed couple as their marriage dissolves and they move slowly through the process of separation and divorce. It has a number of parallels with *Y Tŵr*, particularly its relentless focus on the couple and their implicit isolation from the society around them. Left alone together, the pair speak words that can only echo within the bare walls of their apartment, moving the audience with the sharpness of their observation of the emotional consequences of the break-up, but also creating a world devoid of any redemption or hope.

The power of Cwmni Theatr Cymru's *Alpha Beta* lay largely in the acting performances it elicited from Ogwen and Rhys, which had transformed an effective but unrelentingly joyless play into a theatrical tour de force. This stirred Gwenlyn's interest; and he saw in them a means to create a play which could capitalize on the fact that, along with being two of the most capable professional actors in Wales, they were also a married couple themselves. And so, though the raw experience and imagery for *Y Tŵr* was already at his disposal, the availability of these particular actors was a vital theatrical prerequisite for its creation. He popped the question to them during the National Eisteddfod in Wrexham in 1977: they gleefully accepted. It became one of their most renowned projects, and their collaboration was partly responsible for the play's remarkable longevity in the Welsh public's imagination. (Such was its impact, indeed, that they were invited to revisit the text for a new adaptation of the play in 1995, under the direction of Graham Laker.)

As noted in the introduction, the basic premise of the action is that a man and a woman enter the Tower of the title in their youth, and ascend from one floor to another as they move through their lives together. The rigorous determinism of this three-phase, three-act structure appealed to Parry; but when he first outlined it to his colleague John Hefin, it was not well received. Ever honest, Hefin noted that he thought the whole thing too simplistic: he was given the shortest of shrift in reply. Rendering lived experience into dramatic schema was, after all, Gwenlyn's stock-in-trade, and he had a feeling for this one. Happily, the two men's friendship remained solid.

In one sense, the Tower as a theatrical structure leading an everyman figure through life and up towards his celestial reward is as old as the morality plays of the Middle Ages. However, Parry's imposition of contemporary theatrical conventions (a box-set and fourth-wall televisual realism) on this structure imposes strict limits on the way in which the action is presented and on the way in which the audience witness it. While watching the play we are constantly aware that the action is located in a Tower, but we are never able to see that Tower as an edifice (any more than we are able to see ourselves in the real world around us); and we never hear the characters themselves describing its exterior or its location. Similarly, though we hear the characters referring generically to their own society and environment – their workplaces, their immediate family members and so on – we are never shown those places or those people who exist outside the Tower. In that sense, our perspective on the action is completely interiorized, and we ascribe that same feeling of interiority and incarceration to the characters. Another important effect of Parry's definition of the Tower as an edifice is that it provides no visual evidence of the characters' progress during the play: although we accept that their life together takes them up the Tower from floor to floor, the stage set presents only a single space which always looks the same. What we are shown is a continuous present condition, which leaves no trace of itself in the space around it, and is thus alienated from its own environment: the passage of the individual subject through life and towards death makes no difference to the world around him.

The Tower is far more than just a symbolic location, then; it is a means of shaping and reducing the lives of those within it and of defining the perspective of those outside it, looking in. Moreover, it changes its significance and its effect on the characters and the audience as the play progresses. Far more than the workshop of *Saer Doliau*, the beach shack in *Tŷ ar y Tywod*, or the hovel in *Y Ffin*, the Tower actively moulds the lives caught within it, limiting their potential to be other than they are, deadening and ultimately ossifying them. However, even as it does so, it reveals to those outside – the audience – its full capacity as a vehicle for transforming the banality of everyday life into a pervasive, poetic dread. It has a permanent residual presence, then; a kind of (malign) intelligence, which gradually comes to constitute and be associated with the notion of biography as a force defining, containing, constricting – and eventually replacing – the characters' independent volition.

The audience is confronted with the Tower's 'intelligence' from the outset. When the curtain rises, the stage is empty and dark. '*A green light strengthens on the window to give the impression that the light is flooding the room. In the same way, music is heard. This is not natural music in the true sense of the word but some kind of sequence of abstract sounds, stirring and otherworldly.*'[2] Before the characters appear, we are invited to watch this empty and dark set gradually animating itself through the use of music and lighting; preparing itself, in effect, for the appearance of human subjects. The window (which is in fact a projection screen) dissolves and is replaced by a film sequence of children playing on a beach, 'gambolling among the waves like two young foals'.[3] When the Girl and Boy eventually appear on stage, we complete the implicit link between them and the filmed images, and regard them as living manifestations of the children on the screen; but we cannot ignore the fact that it is the Tower which has shown all this to us, and in so doing, has already made itself a more immediate presence for us than the characters who enter it.

It continues to impress itself onto our awareness as the action proceeds. It supplies the audience with images on the projection screen at various points in the play, pointedly reminding us of significant incidents from the characters' past; it also generates the sounds and voices of unseen others – mainly children – which, according to the characters, seem to emanate from the floors above and below. However, the most obviously 'intelligent' component of the Tower is the staircase, which is conspicuously placed at the centre of the stage and winds its way upwards out of view. Its

presence, shape and sheer visual impact implies a significant intervention in the action; and Parry himself was insistent that the actors
should move around the room in a way which ensured that they
constantly circled, touched and discussed the significance of the
staircase. It was, he said in an English synopsis of *Y Tŵr* in 1979,
'a very important "character" in the play.'[4]

When they appear, the characters are drawn to the stairs almost
immediately. The Girl enters in a state of excitement and euphoria
('I'm here! . . . At last, I'm here!');[5] but the Boy, who has to be summoned into the room, immediately displays a deep sense of unease
at being removed from the rest of his peer group. He suggests
climbing up to the next floor to get further away from the 'others'
below. This is a reasonable suggestion, but it must be resisted
because of the implicit spatial rules which the Tower imposes (and
because, if played out on a conventional theatre stage, there is
nowhere for him to go):

BOY: It'll be much safer!
GIRL: Listen! Try to understand [. . .]
BOY: The higher the better – far away from everyone . . . no-one to peek.
GIRL: Look! This is where we're meant to be [. . .] and this is where
we have to stay for a while [. . .] well, until we're ready, anyway.
BOY: Ready for what?
GIRL: Well [. . .] I don't know [. . .] but I do know that we're not ready
to go now.[6]

The stairs immediately suggest themselves not as an escape route
from the action, then, but as a means of imposing the constraint of
the Tower on the characters. Once inside the Tower, they cannot
leave, and have nowhere to go except onwards through time.

Amenably enough, time moves on very quickly in the Tower –
indeed, as Parry noted himself, the play takes 'absolute liberty
with the passage of time. Even during a single discussion . . . [the
characters] can age two or three years.'[7] This drastic compression of
time undermines much of the implicit realism of the play, a factor
which, once again, suggests a residual 'intelligence' in the space
which acts upon the characters and the audience. Of course, the

characters' dialogue does adhere to the conventions of realistic (televisual) drama, and largely eschews poetic or philosophical discussion (Dewi Z. Phillips notes the very philosophical significance of this lack of cogent self-analysis):[8] they seem to be a very ordinary, working-class couple from Arfon. But the normative realism of their exchanges is undermined by the fact that many of their scenes are too briefly or inadequately sketched to allow them full expression of their emotional responses to events. Their lives are distorted by the Tower. For example, early in Act I, the Girl goads the Boy for his lack of interest in sex, taunting him for being tied to his mother's apron strings; he becomes enraged and slaps her across the face. This is a shocking moment (more so, quite possibly, in a contemporary staging than in the original), but its effect is quickly overridden by the compression of the whole episode. The Boy is immediately appalled by his action and apologizes, saying that he had 'no idea what came over him', and guiltily protests his feelings towards her: 'I wouldn't hurt you for anything in the world . . . I think the world of you.'[9] After a silence, the Girl stops sobbing and comments on the storm clouds over the nearby mountain, which instigates a rather symbolically-loaded reconciliatory dialogue about the weather. For all that it portrays two adolescents in the throes of an immature sexual passion, the conflict is still resolved far more quickly than the audience's capacity to assimilate it. The Tower smoothes over the hurt, and rushes them on to their next scene (in which the storm breaks, and the Girl rushes into the Boy's arms for safety).

On the face of it, this kind of device might seem to be a flaw in terms of the play's pacing; but its effects reveal it to be a part of the Tower's intervention into the characters' lives and a crucial aspect of its reduction of their emotional condition to a simple series of steps in a biographical narrative. It strongly suggests an erasure of memory – that the Girl is capable of forgiving the Boy because her immediate memory of the action is effaced by the compression of time. This is an effect which will be seen to exert an ever-increasing dramatic force as the characters grow older, and will leave the audience as the only consistent and faithful witnesses to their lives. Another important effect arising from the example above is the genericization of the characters' actions, which are transformed from specific instances of feeling into typified gestures of emotion. The characters' actions do not express their individual volition in full, and resemble no more than standard moves in a kind of 'game'. This was precisely the way in which Parry defined them in his English synopsis of the play: in Act I, he noted, the Girl and Boy's 'adolescent game' involves 'talk about sex, other girl/boy friends. They will also argue and fight and talk about their fear of death etc.'[10] Thus, they forgive each other after their quarrel simply because that is what young people tend to do.

The genericization of the action is greatly aided by the use of the projection screen. During Act I, it is deployed several times to reduce the events to commonplace (even clichéd) indices of youth: for example, the Boy imagines what he would look like with a moustache, whereupon the screen duly obliges by showing him sporting several different types; he also fantasizes about owning a motorbike, at which point the screen visualizes his reverie as if it were a television advertisement.[11] Even the couple's most intimate moment, the act of lovemaking, is rendered generic and presented as a kind of instant stereotype by its division between live action on stage and pre-recorded image on screen. On stage, it is stylized, formal and minimal: '*After stepping out of her dress she walks slowly towards the Boy. He does not turn to look at her. She stands by the box for a moment, then lies down on it next to the Boy. After a moment of silence the two of them, simultaneously, turn to face each other and embrace.*' On screen, the act is more graphically portrayed but '*in slow-motion, with the mixing from one shot to another suggesting an almost balletic kind of movement.*'[12] It is obviously a moment which needs to be handled with a certain delicacy: but its division between stage and screen splits it up into two separate visual styles which are jarringly at odds with each other. It also suggests that this moment of intimacy is in fact as much a matter of fantasy as of reality; and this is entirely appropriate to the way in which the couple are divorced from the substance of their lives by the imperative of producing images for the consumption and gratification of the audience.

The Girl's pregnancy precipitates the couple's move up the stairs to the next floor. In Act I, this movement constitutes a leap into the unknown, but it is also the moment at which their relationship becomes formalized. They had previously talked about 'making arrangements', whilst the Girl stood on the stairs, threatening to ascend; but at the time, the Boy shied away from the consequences of this formalization and pleaded instead for an opportunity to seize each moment of pleasure as it comes, and enjoy it to the full: '(*Drawing her to him*) . . . let's make the most of what we've got for a while [. . .] taste everything while we get the chance . . . two hearts beating [. . .] the blood coursing through our veins [. . .] crackling firewood and a sudden shower of rain on a hot day [. . .] loving till it hurts [. . .] hurting till it's love'.[13] The Girl, however, cannot reciprocate this feeling as her condition means that she is already implicated in the nurturing of another life. She has to put her own immediate gratification to one side, and be ready to take her pleasures where she may among her imminent responsibilities. That is what the movement up the stairs means for her. For the Boy, too, it implies a (grudging) acceptance of duty and a fear of loneliness rather than a positive development and deepening of his affection for the Girl:

> (*The Girl slowly climbs the stairs. He does not move, but gazes at her with fear and trepidation. Half way up the stairs, she turns to look at him. The Boy puts his foot on the lowest step and then slowly begins to ascend. When he reaches the Girl, they take each other's hand and then walk, hand in hand, up the stairs. Both of them look fearful and uncertain. Before they reach the top, there is a blackout and the curtains are lowered.*)[14]

This denial of the primacy of pleasure is a major feature of the Tower, and becomes increasingly apparent during Act II of the play. There, along with a physical transformation of the characters into a middle-aged Man and Woman, there is a significant change in the way in which the two characters relate to each other. They are now involved in the 'game of middle age', of professional ambition, '[q]uarrels, suspicions, accusations of unfaithfulness etc.'.[15] The Man now focuses his desire for gratification on his job;

when he enters the action at the beginning of the Act, he appears brash and confident, flushed with social success following dinner with his manager, and believing that he is marked for promotion. His wife, unlike the euphoric Girl whom we saw at the beginning of the play, curses her folly in climbing the stairs so soon in life: 'What the hell am I doing here? . . . If only I'd have listened . . . Bloody hasty'.[16] Accordingly, when she hears the sound of a train in the distance, she interprets it in a way which befits her frustration and melancholy:

> WOMAN: There's something sad about the sound of a train – far away in the night.
> MAN: Sad?
> WOMAN: Saying goodbye [. . .] tears [. . .] going somewhere – leaving!
> MAN: (*after a pause*) Maybe they're arriving [. . .] coming home!
> WOMAN: I never thought of it that way.[17]

The audience, of course, will remember that she has done so in the past. After having made love in Act I, the couple heard the sound of a train passing in the distance, and the Girl was markedly cheered by it: 'There's something nice about the sound of a train far away in the night.'[18] At that time, the train was indicative of a journey into a happy unknown, laden with possibilities; now it is burdened with the awareness that what has been given can be taken away: life is a journey of pain and trepidation rather than pleasure. The fragility of the characters' memory is once again emphasized, but the way in which that fact is presented here shows a distinct development from Act I: there, the erasure of memory was implied by the play's excessive pace and compression of time; here, the characters have forgotten something which we as an audience are very likely to remember, and so, as Elan Closs Stephens has suggested, we begin to regard ourselves as being more adept at creating continuity out of the characters' lives than they are themselves.[19] Our proficiency as their biographers is increasing, and will do so until the end of the play. Our act of spectatorship – together with the structure of the Tower – will continually emphasize the linear narrative progression of their lives, until, by our insistence on completing their story, we drive them on to their end. We will be complicit in the relentless progress of their degeneration.

The second half of Act II provides something of a break from that gradual pattern of deterioration, however. The Man, who has been seen at first to have invested so much of his self-esteem in his work, is now – in later middle age and with failing health – made redundant, while the Woman is hired by his former employer as a nurse. He complains bitterly about the fact that his wife is now the breadwinner of the house, and bemoans the humiliation of his redundancy not only in terms of work but also as a man. As the Woman leaves for the factory, the Man suddenly presents her with evidence of her long-term infidelity with his former boss. The scene is marked by its length – it is by far the most prolonged, unified scene in the play – but also by the way in which the Man is given the means by which to surprise not only his wife but the audience as well. We are shown the incriminating objects (namely the boss's wallet, a photograph and hotel receipts found in her bag) at the same time as the Woman, and we, like her, have had no prior warning of their discovery. In that sense, the scene serves to em-power the Man very significantly, and to foreground his rage to the point where it seems utterly unconstrained by the compressive mechanics and genericizing devices of the Tower. It concludes with an ugly and somewhat triumphantly violent attack on the Woman which brings him to the very depths of despairing self-loathing: 'I'm no good for anything, am I? . . . not even for my wife.'[20] He turns his back on her, and climbs the stairs. Suddenly realizing what he is doing, she rises from her dazed state and pleads with him to wait. He *'pays her no attention, but only carries on walking up slowly but determinedly'*.[21] She follows him, as if broken.

As a scene, the second half of Act II feels like a catharsis, whereas the rest of the play does not. Its sheer force – which has been pre-figured by moments such as the Man of the House's triumph at the end of *Tŷ ar y Tywod*, and which would be seen again in Parry's final play, *Panto* – must cause us to question whether it (and, by implication, the whole play) can be read in a metaphysical sense, as a metaphor which presents a philosophical description of the general hopelessness of the human condition. It seems far more appropriate to suggest a pathological reading, in which the Tower-breaking energy of the Man's fury constitutes a response to repressed anxieties and anger in Gwenlyn's own life.

But the play continues beyond this point of catharsis, a fact which makes its continuity fascinating and problematic. It is significant that, at the time of writing *Y Tŵr*, Gwenlyn himself had occupied only two of the three floors which correspond to the stages in life in his play and, once taken beyond the confines of his own lived experience, the play changes. There is a substantial discrepancy between the vision expressed in the first two Acts of the play and in Act III, with a rather implausible softening of the characters' attitude towards each other, and occasional changes in the manner of Parry's writing. The recent death of his father had no doubt sharpened his awareness of the dreadful finality of that topmost room, but, still, the kind of society which he portrayed in it was not his own. Rather, it was the world of his parents' generation.

Act III follows on directly from the end of the previous scene, and shows us the couple's first entry into the highest room of the Tower. By doing so, it gives us the memorable theatrical shock of seeing the two of them (suddenly) transformed into an elderly couple. The Old Man is weak and breathless after the climb:

> OLD WOMAN: Are you all right?
> OLD MAN: (*without turning his head*) You came, did you?
> OLD WOMAN: (*approaching him in order to sit by his side*) I told you not to rush didn't I?
> OLD MAN: *You* took your time, anyway.
> OLD WOMAN: (*She sits next to her husband*) Those stairs get longer every time.[22]

They are still the same characters in essence, and their words can be read as a reaction to the fact that the (now) Old Man had previously left his wife to climb the stairs on her own. But, of course, we are witnessing a far more substantial transformation than we have seen before. Their physical nature has changed a great deal – they are now far weaker and more vulnerable as characters than they were before, and this undoubtedly changes the audience's attitude towards them. Even more importantly, perhaps, their physical appearance is now completely different, and this forces us to change the way in which we suspend our disbelief and interpret the action. Whereas in the previous acts, the characters were defined by their actions and attitudes, they are now defined by their costume and make-up, which form a kind of 'mantle' about the actors (a fact tacitly admitted by Parry himself, in effect, when the Old Man takes off the trappings of his aged characterization at the end of the act).

As a result, Act III proceeds as a curiously disjointed combination of dramatic continuity and theatrical discontinuity. There is a kind of continuation of the conflict between the characters: in spite of the more conciliatory nature of their relationship in old age, and their evident compassion towards each other as they face their own mortality, there are moments that suggest that the anger which the Old Man felt at the end of Act II is still strong, that it had been temporarily subsumed rather than forgotten. It resurfaces as the Old Man's faculties begin to decline and yields to the final degeneration of his mind. In keeping with the play's treatment of the effacing of memory, he becomes increasingly confused and begins to insist on completely contrary views of past events. Although muddled, however, he is still clearly the same Man in terms of his adherence to the consequences of the life which we have seen him lead on the lower floors. He revisits those events in Act II which had caused him such anguish and anger: it was he, he boasts, who beat off the competition and won promotion at work; it was he who subsequently led his fellow workers out on strike and defiantly gave up his job; and, far from being cuckolded, it was he who rebuffed an attempt by a female colleague to seduce him.

In all of these respects, there is continuity. However, in other ways, particularly in the style and context of the dialogue, there is a distinct discontinuity. The Man's failing memory is first introduced in a comic episode in which he recounts the story of an old acquaintance, Dic (or Wil) Fflat, in which an English tourist is given a memorably nonsensical answer to his request for directions by

the virtually monoglot native: 'How many more miles to Llanberis?'
. . . 'No sea, no mountain, a metalled road all the way.'[23] Although
one of its chief functions as a story is to give a deceptively comic
dimension to the enfeeblement of the Old Man's memory (he barks
at his wife for repeating everything that he says; she retorts, saying
that she is in fact prompting him: ' – I'm saying it before you!'), its
effect is to suggest a milieu far closer to that of Gwenlyn's parents
than his own. The context and the Welsh idiom of the story – indeed,
the very recourse to this kind of folksy storytelling – belong to an
age utterly incompatible with that of the couple we have witnessed
in previous acts. Several other comments and stories, such as the
Old Man's memory of his father cleaning his smoking pipes by
boiling them in a saucepan on the Monday after Thanksgiving,
have a similarly anachronistic quality.

Given the proximity of the writing of this play to the death of
his own father, it is hardly surprising to see Parry taking a conciliatory approach to the portrayal of the elderly. But the kind of
disjunction which we see in this Act has more to it than that. The
replacement of the tempestuousness of Act II with the more amenable, kindly disposition of Act III constitutes a kind of retreat from
harsh reality; and it mirrors the characters' own dilemma in the
final stages of the play, where they too deviate from reality into
fantasy as a means of trying to alleviate the pain of facing death.
The Old Woman has been eager to ensure that the two of them
should be honest with each other as they face their final infirmities.
Back in Act I, she expressed her distress and disgust at the 'game'
which she had played with her own mother as she lay dying of
cancer, in which she attempted to comfort her with bogus stories
of 'summer holidays which would never come' in order to avoid
facing and discussing her terminal condition. Desperate to avoid
such a situation in her own case, she has urged her husband to
promise to tell her 'The truth [. . .] always the truth' and, if necessary, to assist her to a dignified end.[24] He has agreed: however, as
he sickens and nears death, it is he – prompted to some extent by
his wife – who begins to indulge the same evasive fantasy:

OLD WOMAN: You'll get over this (*Pause*) [. . .]
OLD MAN: Before summer, d'you mean?
OLD WOMAN: Oh [. . .] definitely before summer [. . .]
OLD MAN: (*After a long pause*) I'd like some proper holidays this year [. . .] somewhere we've never been.
OLD WOMAN: Like where?
OLD MAN: I don't know [. . .] somewhere that's good and hot [. . .] 'til the top of your head fries [. . .] like that place we went to before [. . .] d'you remember? [. . .] Toro [. . .] you remember [. . .] (*Trying to remember the word*) Toro [. . .]
OLD WOMAN: Toromolinos.[25]

She becomes further implicated in the game of denial when he asks her to administer a lethal dose of morphine in order to bring his suffering to an end. As has been the case throughout the play, the request is made implicitly rather than directly, and its effect described – even as she injects him – as a medicinal treatment, as a matter of comfort and relief rather than death. The Old Man lies back and lapses into a final unreality:

OLD MAN: And if it's fine in Toromolinos [. . .] we'll lie all day by that old swimming pool [. . .] (*He lies back*) [. . .] A dirty big glass of Bacardi and Coke [. . .] a two-hundred packet of fags – duty free [. . .] and the sun [. . .] shining [. . .] warm [. . .] fine [. . .] on my belly . . . [26]

The Old Man's death is, of course, followed by his resurrection. This scene has – obviously – been interpreted as a typically Gwenlynian gesture of hope at the end of the play, following on from the famous *coup* of the ringing telephone at the end of *Saer Doliau*. But the image is far more ambiguous and inconclusive. The words that the Man speaks as he climbs the stairs are largely a repetition of ones which he uttered in Act I while begging for an opportunity to hold on to youth a little longer, to seize every experience and to live life to the full: 'Let's get out of this place [. . .] out into the fresh air [. . .] tasting it all while we we've got a chance [. . .] do you hear me? Two hearts beating [. . .] loving until it hurts [. . .] hurting until it's love.'[27] As such, they have the familiar quality of a memory replayed about them (such as we have already seen through the use of the projection screen, which is used here again); and several commentators have described them, and indeed the whole episode, as images played out in the mind of the Old Woman rather than an assertion of life after death. In addition, although their poetic idealism is heady, the Man's words should not blind us to the fact that, when they were first spoken in Act I, they were hardly sincere, being merely an underlying expression of fear at the consequences of moving on up the Tower; even then, the hope they expressed was entirely futile, as the journey to the next stage had been irreversibly precipitated by the Girl's pregnancy.

One image remains: and it is one which brings us back to the question posed in the introduction: what does the Tower mean? As an unseen force, a latent 'intelligence', it might be said to have affinities with the idea of God, with the idea of a higher being who somehow influences, frames and shapes human experiences. However, as Dewi Z. Phillips might argue, it is a notion of God from which man is completely alienated, in the same way in which he appears to be alienated from his fellow beings on earth. A more persuasive – and biographically apt – possibility is that, as a constraining, punishing force, it corresponds to the Freudian superego; and the increasing anguish which it exerts as the play progresses is the personal, psychological pain of repression, of a crushed libido. In that sense, it is entirely consistent with Parry's previous plays: they had all been concerned, in their dramatic schema and their theatrical manifestation, with the relationship between the superego as an inhibiting force and the capriciousness of the free energies of the id. The threat of the cellar creature in *Saer Doliau*, the monstrous eruption of the fairground at the end of *Tŷ ar y Tywod*, and the descent into animality at the end of *Y Ffin* were all manifestations of the same persistent conflict, and a kind of self-imposed punishment for attempting to assert his predilection for fantasy through the creative power of theatre.

The final image of *Y Tŵr*, however, does not come from within the Tower – from within that superegotistical structure – but from the outside. The Old Woman, after wondering aloud what the purpose of the journey through life might have been, is given a cryptic answer: the sound of a train in the distance. As already noted, it has been heard twice before: after the couple had made love in Act I, at which point the Girl felt comforted by it, and early in Act II, where it is associated with the melancholia of the Woman's disaffection. Here, at the end of the play, the sound brings the Old Woman some kind of brief happiness ('*A little smile appears on the Old Woman's face.*'),[28] as if to suggest that she herself now has a journey to undertake, or that she has achieved a kind of final acceptance of her life in its totality. The exact significance of the image is, as ever, left open to interpretation; but the repeated us of the device of the train throughout the play certainly suggests an underlying continuity. And though the Woman may not be consciously aware of the fact that she has heard the sound on previous occasions, it never fails to move her one way or another.

What is most important about the image of the train is that it is as persistent as the Tower itself, but is utterly free. It has no part in the Tower's force of constraint – indeed, it is radically opposed to it: it is mobile, the Tower static; it journeys through the world in the horizontal plane, the Tower is oppressively vertical. It rivals the Tower, and is in stark contrast to it. If we can accept that the Tower possesses the characteristics of the superego, then, the train corresponds neatly to the Freudian notion of a drive. It is somewhat alien, unknown and in constant motion, and thus accords with the sense of a basic motivating force within the individual's psychophysical composition. It rushes blindly '*through the dark to somewhere*', and thus retains a feeling of independent, capricious volition. It has no memory, no biography, and constitutes all that remains unaffected, unclaimed by the Tower.

But there is another aspect to the train as a final image in the play too. It constitutes a fleeting awareness of a presence, or a promise, of something after death, far more than the rather literal image of the Man's resurrection. In that sense, it is entirely consistent with Gwenlyn's own desire that he should hear or feel something from his father after his demise, and with his further belief in the potential for communication beyond the known. Its inclusion at this point in his writing, at this culminating moment of his most powerful and successful play, serves to sum up the role that writing for the theatre had held for him throughout his career until this point. On one hand it had been an act of memorialization, an attempt to honour and temporarily re-animate the world in which he had been born and raised, by the restaging of its language, its manners and mores. But it had also been a direct attempt to communicate with something beyond common understanding, and, by theatrical means, to suggest – more in hope than expectation – that there was an audience out there to hear and observe the plight of the human subject and to give it some kind of final acknowledgement on its journey through and out of life.

With Y Tŵr, all had now been said and done. It was a play which had revisited a number of aspects of his early work but dispensed with the kind of abstraction which had led him to locate them in an allegorical void. Here, Parry brought his drama far closer to the contemporary world, setting it in an edifice which, although it was isolated from society, allowed its inhabitants nonetheless to be subject to current influences and attitudes. By moving on from his trilogy, Parry had come out of that fragile and rather pitiful shell which he had erected around the main subjects in those plays. It was a move which was to change his work – and his life – in a number of different ways.

Among the various responses to Y Tŵr (reviews of the production were, once again, not universally favourable), the one which Parry treasured most of all was the glowing introduction to the published version given by Saunders Lewis, in which he described Parry as a 'poet of a dramatist, pretending to be a B.B.C. man'.[29] This was a plaudit which Parry jokingly lauded in the company of friends, often repeating the line from Y Tŵr which Lewis had quoted in his introduction as evidence of poetic craft – "Di 'di dechra' ta?' ['Has it started then?']. Though it meant a great deal to him, in company he would treat it with a rather coy mock-condescension, marvelling that one so learned could stoop to consider the scribblings of a council house boy from Llanbabo.

This was a typically ambivalent attitude towards criticism of his work. According to several of his colleagues, he was quite content to accept critical comment, favourable or otherwise; but only if he trusted the source. And, if he was somewhat reticent to comment at length on his work, he was keenly aware of what was said about it: interviews and discussions of his playwriting often saw him making general reference to the ideas and opinions of critics. Interestingly, however, he often referred to critics' opinions with the same mock condescension with which he greeted Saunders Lewis's celebration of his work. Critical opinions were often phrased as matters of authority ('critics tell me that my work is . . . '; 'they say that I . . . '), which conferred upon them an ironically elevated status and honour, as if the critics, *bien sur*, could always see what the poor artist could not. At other times, he voiced a rather weary dismissal of critical prattle. For example, when asked by a television interviewer to comment on the theory, suggested by some, that the element of menace in his plays arose from a residual memory of his father's dangerous profession as a quarryman, Gwenlyn replied, 'That's what they say . . . ', before adding, with a mischievous gleam in his eye, 'I don't care for most of them.'[30]

His exposure to criticism had increased over the years due to the expansion of his activity as a writer and script editor at the BBC. As if in return, he tried to ensure that those within the corporation whose efforts might end up in the public eye were thoroughly nurtured and supported. After the successes of the early and mid-1970s, Parry was promoted to senior script editor – or head of scripting – and was now a figure who set the agenda for others to follow. Accordingly, he cultivated a number of 'apprentices', several of whom became close personal acquaintances and admirers, such as William Jones – who succeeded Gwenlyn as script editor on *Pobol y Cwm* – Sion Eirian and Dewi Wyn Williams (it was these three, along with Meic Povey, who bore Parry's coffin in 1991).[31] Being an apprentice of this kind was not only a question of sharing the same vocation or commitment to writing and drama production: it was also a matter of sharing the same temperament, and most certainly the same capacity for *hwyl*. The culture of the BBC Club, first at Broadway, then at the new centre in Llandaff, became legendary in this respect. Gwenlyn and Rhydderch positioned themselves as rulers of a court, which was as dedicated to bohemianism as it was to creativity, and included such noble institutions as the *Celwrn* and the Friday afternoon 'Poet's Day' ['Piss off early, tomorrow's Saturday'].[32] Sion Eirian – one of the young writers whom Parry brought into the scripting team for *Pobol y Cwm* and who subsequently went on to have a long and successful career as a writer for stage and screen – described the BBC Club as an 'outpost of creativity one step removed from the BBC Centre', in which a kind of productive indiscipline was rife. But if indiscipline it was, it was sanctioned by innovation and effort: although there may have been a relaxing of expectations concerning when and how the creative work of the Scripting Department was to be achieved, there was no compromise on the fact that it *was* to be achieved. Moreover, notes Eirian, this was a period in which the individual voice of the writer (or writing team) was more crucial: television had not yet fallen prey to the deadening determinism of the fixed format, and, in that respect, the intensity of the writing and production culture was crucial: 'We would fall asleep against each other at the end of the day', he noted of life at the club. 'The feeling of being a family, even physically so, was very real.'[33]

Gwenlyn's influence in the BBC began to shift during this time, with his editorial function taking greater precedence over his role as a writer. He was increasingly a motivator and facilitator, rather than a writer in his own right; and this, according to Sion Eirian, became one of his most important legacies. As a result of the various cultural upheavals of the later 1970s (such as punk and Thatcherism, to name but two), tastes and influences – even in Wales – were changing, and innovations in programme formats and design meant that the drive to renew ideas about the preferred rules and conventions of television drama was constant. Parry's younger colleagues had interests and preoccupations which were often significantly at variance with his own; but he was seriously committed to the task of allowing them to develop their own ideas and establish their own voices as writers.

8

'You know who's in the balance?': *Sal*

The extent to which Parry was preoccupied with his role as a facilitator for the development of Welsh television drama may well be seen from the form and fate of his next stage play, *Sal*. It would be fair to describe it as Parry's 'forgotten' play: originally conceived around 1970, it had been intended as a television drama, with John Hefin as producer, and then as a radio play; but it was never seen through to full production, and remained 'in planning' for a decade. When it was finally produced as a stage play in 1980 by Cwmni Theatr Cymru, it received what was generally agreed to be a lacklustre first production, and its publication two years later attracted no great acclaim. It has not been restaged since.

In many ways, this was hardly Gwenlyn's fault. The production was in trouble even before it began rehearsal. Cwmni Theatr Cymru had never intended to stage *Sal* at this point. They had planned and commissioned a production of Saunders Lewis's controversial television play *Excelsior*, and Lewis had been working on a stage version since about April 1979, in time for production during March and April 1980. However, *Excelsior* had been banned on charges of libel after its first broadcast in 1962, and, contrary to the company's (possibly rather naive) expectations, it suddenly appeared that it could well be banned again. Upon receipt of legal advice, Cwmni Theatr Cymru's board decided that *Excelsior* could not go ahead: news of the decision broke on the 8 January 1980 (much to Lewis's dismay, as he had not been forewarned), and *Sal* was quickly earmarked to take its place. It is hard to discern when exactly Parry was brought into the process of providing a replacement play for Lewis's production, but the decision to adapt *Sal* rather than write a completely new play may well have had something to do with the haste which the commission from Cwmni Theatr Cymru now demanded. In any case, however prepared Parry's script was, it was produced in an atmosphere of no little turmoil in terms of rearranging casting and production schedules to accommodate the new work.

Sal (1980)

The fact that *Sal* was adapted from an existing concept makes it rather difficult to locate the play chronologically in a consideration of Parry's work for the stage. It does share some features and thematic characteristics of his previously produced and published play *Y Tŵr*, but it is in many ways closer to his earlier works; and, in a sequential study of the stage plays, a case could certainly be made to look at it between *Tŷ ar y Tywod* (which it mirrors and develops in a number of respects) and *Y Ffin*. However, and crucially, examining *Sal* after *Y Tŵr* allows us to consider the way in which the play was received by the public and the way in which its stage production affected Parry's reputation as a theatre writer. *Sal* suffered in comparison with *Y Tŵr*: it was not as well crafted a play for the stage, and the fact that it had originally been written for television undermined aspects of its effectiveness in the theatre. Moreover, it was also seen as distinctly un-Gwenlynian: it placed its scenes in a number of different locations – the first time that he had done so in his stage plays since *Poen yn y Bol*; it was based on historical events, rather than in the realm of the imagination; and it was also, even at the time of its first performance, somewhat dated. Although less than ten years had elapsed since its original conception, the Welsh audience had changed considerably in terms of its values and tastes; and so *Sal* was cut adrift from the milieu in which it had been created. This is important, because Parry's status as a dramatist had been associated not only with his capacity to raise challenging metaphysical questions through his plays but also with his capacity to embody something of the zeitgeist in his theatricality.

However, there are aspects of *Sal* that do demonstrate a sense of continuity with his previous work. It is fundamentally consistent with his interest in familial life, religion and the presence of the ineffable; and there is a distinct parallel between the quality of mystery in *Sal* and the rather enigmatic final image of *Y Tŵr*. Both seem to be concerned with the way in which a human life might be receptive to, and become a conduit for, phenomena beyond ordinary comprehension. Also like *Y Tŵr*, *Sal*'s dramaturgy was influenced by the techniques of television drama, and was far more episodic in its structure than his earlier stage plays. This episodic structure had also been an important underlying feature of *Y Tŵr*, but it was largely masked by the fact that the Tower's compression of time and concentration of the action into a single location forcibly imposed a kind of unity on the action. With *Sal*, the episodic structure was far more apparent, based on the play's consistent use of flashback as a device for organizing the action.

The play concerns the case of Sarah Jacob, 'the miraculous fasting girl' of Llethr-Neuadd near Pencader in Carmarthenshire during the late 1860s. Her story attracted great attention at that time, and has remained a matter of curiosity, if not mystery, ever since. It was claimed that Sarah, known to her family as Sal, had refused all food and drink for two years, and that her survival during this period was evidence of a divine intervention. Reports of her condition, which became described as a 'miracle', reached the media and thence the public, who flocked to Llethr-Neuadd to look at her and be in her presence. In due course, medical personnel were dispatched in order to verify the claim that Sal was eating and drinking nothing. Shortly after the medical observation began, however, and still refusing all means of sustenance, she began to ail: she died a few days later, and her death resulted in a court case against her parents for manslaughter.

In spite of the considerable differences between *Sal* and Parry's other major stage plays – and in spite of the fact that it had been conceived for television – the theatricality of the play cannot be denied. *Sal* is, at its very heart, a work for the stage, and can only really find its true expression in front of a live audience. It is concerned with religious belief as a revelatory event, one which transforms and colours an individual's experience; it is also concerned with the mutable and problematic manifestation of the experience of belief through language. Rather like *Tŷ ar y Tywod*, *Sal*'s central device proposes a miraculous animation, the creation and transformation of a Žižekian 'autonomous partial object', and it takes full advantage of theatre's capacity to bring a concept or proposition to life before an audience – for those willing to suspend disbelief, at least. Sal's miraculous endurance is achieved by persuading the audience to accept the suggestion of her survival, in precisely the same way that the Dummy in *Tŷ ar y Tywod* is animated not just by the Man of the House's fantastical desire for her but also by the audience's fundamental predisposition to believe that which is proposed to them as part of the stage world.

Sal reflects *Tŷ ar y Tywod* in several ways. In effect, it takes the conflict between the Fair Owner and the Man of the House, and their respective assertions or denials that the Dummy is 'just a thing', and extends them throughout the whole play. By doing so, it repeats the trick that was central to the earlier play, and sets two key aspects of theatre against each other: its representative function, through which experience is replicated and reported by means of dialogue and scene-setting, and its transformational function, through which an audience is invited to believe that something powerful and transcendent may become present in the moment of theatrical exposure. The action is generated by the constant juxtaposition of these two functions – the detached, quasi-scientific observation of reconstituted action and the implicated immersion into belief; or, as Rhydderch Jones notes in his introduction to the play, by the interplay between 'faith and anatomical fact, between the Word and words'.[1]

The conflict between these two functions is suggested even in the opening tableau of the play. Sal is separated and distinguished from the rest of the characters, illuminated and fully visible to the audience as they take their seats. Once the audience has settled, the other characters – including the Prosecutor and Counsel for the Defence, as well as the Father and Mother, Evan and Hannah

Jacob – take their places around the bed, with their backs turned to the auditorium. In turn, they begin to speak, addressing the audience directly with their various introductory statements, but Sal remains silent. She is presented as an icon, while the other characters (whether they believe in her miraculous condition or not) are presented as discursive subjects to be judged according to the sincerity or persuasiveness of their arguments. The fact that this courtroom setting represents her parents' trial for her man-slaughter means, of course, that Sal cannot directly intervene in these proceedings, and can only be animated by the 'magical' device of flashback. However, even when she does speak, she does not articulate herself to the same extent as the other characters (even her relatively tongue-tied Mother). She is presented as a mystery, her first description of her condition being cryptic, and inexplicable even to herself:

> THE GIRL: Everything is so light sometimes [. . .] so clear [. . .] I can almost touch.
> THE FATHER: What, Sal? [. . .] Touch what? (*The Vicar looks at him reprovingly*)
> THE VICAR: (*Somewhat indifferently*) Touch what, my girl?
> THE GIRL: That's the trouble! I don't know [. . .][2]

Sal feels as if she has been chosen, but cannot say to what end; and the mystery deepens as she suffers a sudden and violent fit because of the presence of food near her bed. All of this serves to define her as an object of fascination, one whose outward form betrays nothing of her complex – inexplicable – inner state. The parallel between Sal as a character and the Dummy in *Tŷ ar y Tywod* is thus a pertinent one: not only are they both manifestations of a kind of miracle, they are both powerfully *objectified*. This aspect is taken up by Gwenan Mared Roberts, in a valuable analysis of *Sal*'s treat-ment of femininity. She emphasizes the way in which Sal is defined by her body, and how that body becomes the site of inquiry and of anxiety.[3] It is objectified from the first, being placed in a state some-where between life and death: Sal is described as lying on her bed, motionless, looking 'as if she could easily be dead' (and it is worth remembering that the speeches which accompany this image discuss her death); but she is also described as having 'a contented little smile on her face' which suggests that she is merely asleep. Her physical adornment also produces a sense of objectification: she has ribbons in her hair, and wears white gloves, which, Gwenan Mared argues, may be a sly reference to the Victorian aphorism describing Wales as *hen wlad y menyg gwynion*, 'the old land of the white gloves'. This was a sentimentalized claim of purity, made in defence of the nation's honour against the accusations of the 1847 Blue Books, but it created very narrow parameters for morality and set the bar for hypocrisy – particularly sexual hypocrisy – at an unfeasibly low level. It is this sexual hypocrisy, she argues, which is at the core of the play. Her analysis has a great deal to recommend it, and Sal's white gloves certainly do suggest a (possibly rather too overt) preoccupation with purity, and a symbolic sense of her body as an object of veneration and anxiety. Her physical state resembles that of the Man of the House in its aversion to contact, and indicates a rather surgical preference for a barrier between the self and the hostile outside world. But it is important to note that Sal's words, quoted above, also suggest that she is seeking the experience of touch, and that her gloves could be seen not just as a barrier against the world but also as an impediment to her desire for contact with it. She is objectified, but, like the Dummy, she is also fetishized by being imbued with a desire which requires the intervention of external (male) agents in order to be named and expressed.

That fetishization is foregrounded when the Vicar overcomes his initial doubts as to Sal's condition and is persuaded by her miraculous state. He talks to her, listens to her reciting Psalm 23, and holds her hand, whereupon he is overcome by a wondrous sensation: 'I felt [. . .] (*He pauses and looks at the hand that was holding the Girl's*) [. . .] I felt some strange heat shooting from her hand – through me! . . . (*Almost to himself*) Not a natural heat [. . .]'.[4] It is not Sal's words but her touch which has created this sensation in the Vicar; and the sensual, even sexual, connotation of this 'heat' is not incidental. It is pursued and developed throughout the play in the condition of the room around Sal, which – particularly towards the end – is said to be cold, and requires her to preserve her heat, by keeping her hands under the bedclothes or by having them intrusively washed by one of her nurses. The notion of heat is also implicit in the images of fire in the play, which once again have associations with purity and with sexuality. Towards the end of the play, Sal reads the story of the three boys in the fiery furnace from the Book of Daniel, an allusion which actively brings together the idea of 'unnatural' heat, trial by ordeal and the miraculous survival of the body. A similar image – that of 'purgatory' – is used in a sexual context by Nurse Ann, one of the observers sent from Guy's Hospital to verify Sal's condition, when describing her own experience of puberty and the onset of menstruation. This, she argues, may be a contributory factor to Sal's psychological condition. Thus the objectification of Sal is associated not only with a miraculous image of faith undaunted in the face of persecution, but also with the otherness, the inescapable alienness (from a masculine perspective), of the female sexual body.

The play constitutes a probing of that body, and it does so in two ways: first, through the action of the court, whose inquiry into the condition of Sal's body applies different kinds of narrative to her vital processes (psychological, medical and forensic); and secondly, through poetic imagery, which is often associated, particularly in the case of Sal and her Father, with the possibility that Sal may have been sexually abused. This idea is taken up in Gwenan Mared Roberts's analysis of the play, in which she argues that there is an important link between the suggestion of abuse, Sal's self-starvation and the overbearing influence of the Father, Evan Jacob.[5] Sal's condition, she argues, may have been caused by her attempt to regain control of her body following abusive sexual encounters, evidence for which is provided circumstantially throughout the play: through the Father's underlying hostility to invasive questioning and medical examination; through his dismissive treatment of the Mother (whose relative silence during the play thus becomes deeply ominous); and, more importantly in this case, through the use of highly allusive, phallically-loaded Biblical quotation. Roberts makes particular reference to the Father's quotation from Psalm 23, which he uses to encourage Sal, even as her life ebbs away, not to give up her fight to embody the miracle: 'His rod and staff [. . .] remember that, Sal [. . .]'[6] Her argument is persuasively made, because the implications of the imagery cannot be restrained, and, even if it does not directly *reveal* a kind of abuse at the heart of the play, the suggestion surely acts upon the audience's sensibilities, either consciously or unconsciously. However, we must remain circumspect about interpreting *Sal* as a play which concerns a specific issue or conflict which can be revealed readily once the action is divested of its various ambiguities. This is precisely the kind of reasoning which so thoroughly and redundantly preoccupied a number of commentators after *Saer Doliau* and *Tŷ ar y Tywod*

It is this dispute between concrete evidence and imaginative suggestion that drives the action forward. *Sal* is, in effect, two plays in one. It is the courtroom drama which pits the Father and the Defence Counsel against the Prosecutor and the various doctors, and it is also the miraculous drama of Sal's enhancement, her acceptance of that role, and its destruction of her. The play constantly oscillates between these two basic scenarios and their contrasting modes of theatrical presentation, to create a playful, unstable and ambiguous whole. In the courtroom drama, the most evident modes of rhetoric employed are argument and deduction, which correspond to the idea of *logos*, the word as established through investigation and reasoning. This is exemplified by the exchanges between the Counsels and witnesses, particularly (as in the case of Dr Hughes) where the witness is aggressively sceptical of the Jacobs' claims. These create a kind of *agon* of dialogic exchange aimed at the establishing of observable, objective truth. However, although quite objective in its approach, the courtroom drama is neither dispassionate nor unpoetic: it possesses life and humour, and a lyricism of its own – even the quality of a litany at particular points. For example, Dr Hughes's account of the physical processes which give rise to ketosis, although based on scientific rather than lyrical language, becomes imbued on stage with a sensual quality and a horror which is texturally rich; and the recitation of the postmortem findings at the end of the play has a distinctly ceremonial formality and rhythm. On the other hand, the play of Sal's miraculous translation into God's vessel, played out by her, Evan Jacob and the Vicar (throughout most of the play) employ the opposite kind of rhetoric, that of divine revelation, or *mythos*. Here, the causes of an experience are entirely mysterious and circumscribed by the poetry of the moment; thus they do not lead to discursive dialogue, but rather to sequences of poetic affirmation of different kinds – particularly textual allusion (references to the Bible), metaphor and the 'testimony' of the body. For example, as reported by her Father, the initial moment of Sal's revelation is said to have occurred when she visited the local church:

> That's when she noticed [. . .] that's when she felt the thing [. . .] there by the altar [. . .] before His figure on the cross . . . Look in her eyes, Vicar. See how the Divine Light blazes in them. She is in the company of the heavenly ones . . . She knows that the Almighty has chosen her.[7]

The conflict between these two rhetorical 'plays' of *mythos* and *logos* undermines their respective claims to the truth. The Prosecutor and the sceptical Dr Hughes are frequently seen to revel in the power of their own, supposedly dispassionate, rhetoric; and, similarly, Sal is caught up in the performance of her miraculous survival, and becomes complicit in the creation of an aggrandized image of herself. Both become convinced by the potency of their testimony as theatre, and the truth or falsity of their assertions become a secondary matter when compared with the immediate power which their own performance licenses. Rather like the trial scenes in Arthur Miller's *The Crucible*, *Sal* shows how imbuing a performance with life (and life with performance) can create a momentum of its own, and a personal conviction which far outweighs the burden of logical or material proof; all of which leads simultaneously to exultation and disaster. The effect of this image is felt not only in Sal's bedroom, but throughout the whole neighbourhood. When Dr Hughes arrives to examine Sal, he notes that a substantial publicity machine has been assembled around her. The train to

Pencader (the nearest station to Llethr-Neuadd), he says, was uncharacteristically full, and the scene at the station itself was 'worse than Cardigan Fair, it was like a circus [. . .] and these boys on the platform with placards – *"To the Fasting Girl"*, *"This way to Llethr-Neuadd"*. One lad had written *"Guide to the miracle"* on his hat.'[8] Sal has become caught up in this seething momentum, becoming aware of her power as an icon (towards the middle of the play, for example, we see her bedecked in a floral crown and shawl and with an open Bible in her hand). But it is never clear whether she is instigating the hysteria, or whether it is forcing a kind of dramaturgy onto her. In any case, the potency of her performance has become a reality and a kind of truth in itself for her and those thronging to visit her, and, fraudulent or not in terms of its causes, its effects are real. As Jean Duvignaud says with reference to the way in which an audience activates theatrical illusion by its belief in the action: 'for those who *expect* a miracle there is no deceit'.[9]

But Sal's belief in her own miraculous condition seems to wane as the play draws to a conclusion. For Dewi Z. Phillips, this was evidence of the fact that those beliefs were entirely insubstantial, based on an amorphous occultism which could not be mediated through coherent personal language. His complaint is apt enough, but it decries not only *Sal* but the whole of modernist drama: the provoking of powerful sensations out of insubstantiality, and their promotion to the status of reality (albeit a temporary and contingent one) is the very core of that medium. In that sense, we can postulate that Sal does not lose her faith at the end, but rather that the falling narrative arc of the play brings her capacity to be a character to a close. She loses her theatricality, in a manner somewhat akin to Prospero's renunciation of his magical art at the end of Shakespeare's *Tempest*. Even though her decline is horrific (at the last, she finds herself plagued by the odour of burning flowers and bewildered by 'his' – nominally God, although the word is highly ambiguous – abandonment of her), we can accept it as being more 'natural' than the zealous, obsessional steadfastness of the Father, Evan Jacob. He does not witness his daughter's death, but is engrossed in reciting the passages from the Book of Genesis which describe God's intervention in Abraham's attempt to sacrifice his son Isaac. In the Bible story, the death of the child is averted and a ram sacrificed in his place, but in Sal's case there is no reprieve, and the Father, despite a momentary pause in which he feels a pang of grief, continues to recite the story until Dr Davies comes to commiserate with him. As with so much of the action of the play, this concluding passage reads more than one way: the Father may be fully aware of the significance of the moment, and his faith – whether corrupted or not – may be so strong that he does not need to be present at his daughter's end; or it may be weakened, and his repetition of God's words to Abraham may be a means of denying his responsibility for Sal's death. If we accept the first possibility, then we are confronted by the will of God as something (possibly) benign but deeply unknowable: He has not abandoned Sal or the Father, and has indeed intervened, as He did with Abraham; but the manner and meaning of His intervention, which has not spared Sal's life, is beyond all human understanding. If we accept the second possibility, we may either regard the Father as a man in the grip of a delusion, consumed by a false but earnest faith, or as a cynical liar – one who has realized at last that he is responsible for the death of his child, but must maintain the pretence of faith in order to avoid the earthly consequences of his guilt.

All of these possibilities remain active as he confronts the audience at the very end. He attacks the authority of the court and, by extension, the act of judgement which the audience is implicitly asked to conduct in the aftermath of the play:

> Yes, go, it's about time you went, to argue amongst yourselves, to pronounce and pontificate according to your knowledge. But we're not the ones being weighed in the balance here [. . .] you understand that, don't you [. . .] (*He is shouting now*) [. . .] you know who's in the balance?'[10]

His previous Biblical quotation suggest that he means that it is God who is on trial here, and that a judgement made upon God is a sure way to human disaster. But the fact that he does not specifically name God leaves the ending of the play open to other interpretations too: Gwenan Mared Roberts suggests that it is patriarchal masculinity which is on trial.[11] The rhetoric of the scene also suggests very strongly that it is the audience members themselves who are on trial, and in passing judgement on the case, or on the play, they are implicitly passing judgement on themselves. In another sense, it is not only the play but also the act of theatrical presentation that is on trial. With his final words, the character asks the audience to consider what is bound up in the act of representation, and whether that act is capable of being more than just an illustration of a dramatic proposal, or a pretext for a socially-shared entertainment. In effect, he asks whether there is anything fundamental to our lives as human beings in the act of representation. Whatever its relevance to the case of Sarah Jacob, it is the same question which we have found at the heart of Parry's work from the very beginning.

Sal may not have been a play that was planned and executed in the most orderly fashion, and it may be routinely dismissed as something of a footnote to Gwenlyn's career as a 'serious' writer; but it is, nonetheless, a very powerful play in essence. Gwenan Mared Roberts's suggestion that it might be time to reconsider its strengths is well made.[12] In 1980, critical response to *Sal* was relatively muted. Writing in *Y Cymro*, the novelist Eigra Lewis Roberts complimented the production generally for its professionalism and for Parry's treatment of the historical material. However, there was an element of faint praise in her comment, and she expressed some regret that *Sal* did not have a stronger emotional appeal. Responding to the fact that the television version of *Y Tŵr* had attracted criticism from some of the more conservative sectors of the audience, she noted that there could be no room for objection to the language in this play:

> We must give room and welcome to this but we should also give room and welcome to a play like the same author's *Y Tŵr*, a striking play with very strong emotional power. Shouldn't we consider a play as an artistic whole, a live, exciting thing, and not as a moral or academic experiment? It is the striking play which stays with me after I have left the theatre, with its plaguey questioning still swirling in my mind.[13]

Rhydderch Jones, in his introduction to the published version of the play, described it as a fusion of Parry's scientific and medical background and his interest in religion. He reminded the reader that Gwenlyn used to be a lay preacher, and added that he still held true 'to the instruction of the Sunday School and the chapel to this day, with a kind of *hiraeth* which borders on the obsessional.'[14] His comments are valuable in returning the focus of discussion to Parry's own life, and to his attempt to account for his discovery of a vocation in writing. Was his disposition towards drama God-given, or was he merely immersing himself in a self-sustaining, temporary delusion? True to his background as an artist, a preacher and a science teacher, the answer was somehow implicit in the enactment of the experiment, and in the subsequent dispute concerning the interpretation of the findings. But *Sal* is also, like *Y Tŵr*, anti-systematic, and a means by which Parry battles to the last against the objectifying, deterministic authority of theatrical representation as an activity which reduces the human being to a trial exhibit. The Father's attack on the act of judgement at the end of *Sal* is more than just an attack on his prosecutors. It is an attack on the jurors – the audience – and the whole basis of the play. From within the action of the play, he declares himself to be outside its remit and its fundamental form: he is an enraged loose cannon, claiming an authority which is wholly excessive and, and as it has been throughout the play, perilously transgressive. In that respect, the Father as a character fits well into the gap between *Y Tŵr* and Parry's next and final stage play, *Panto*, dominated as it is by its own dynamically irresponsible male lead.

9

'Any bloody fool can play dame': *Panto*

In 1981, the television industry in Wales began to change dramatically following the campaign to fund a Welsh fourth television
channel. Parry had been energetically involved in arguments for
production facilities and in the planning of schedules for the new
channel through his active membership of the group *Undeb Darlled-
wyr Cymru* – the Union of Welsh Broadcasters. The advent of S4C
created more hours for programme makers in Wales to fill, and a
completely new brief to fulfil in terms of making Welsh-language
television a viable cultural proposition. Its increased profile also
meant that it would now have to justify itself as never before, and
the job of nurturing new talent to write for television would become
increasingly urgent. Parry had already moved on from script editing
to take overall charge of scripting at the BBC Drama Department,
and would continue his move from the specifics of programme
making to the creation and implementation of longer-term strat-
egies. In the case of *Pobol y Cwm*, for example, he became the series
producer, and oversaw the expansion of the writing team from
about a dozen writers to more than two dozen.

Alongside all of these adjustments in his professional circumstances, there was a significant change in his personal life too.
Gwenlyn had first met Ann Beynon when she assumed the role of
secretary to Yr Academi Gymreig during the late 1970s. Gradually,
and almost imperceptibly at first, a deep affection grew between
them. The growth of their relationship surprised Gwenlyn: the
very idea that a woman some twenty years younger than him could
become attracted to him was unexpected. But the feeling was mutual,
and, after some time, he could no longer deny the feelings that he had

for Ann. His life was thrown into no little turmoil: he was beset by intense feelings of guilt, aware that breaking up his marriage to Joye would also be a breach of his role as a parent. Leaving would involve a cruel betrayal of trust.

He discussed his emotions with several very close colleagues during this time – a practice which a number of them have described as uncharacteristic, Gwenlyn being comparatively silent about his innermost feelings. He found support among some, but disapproval and even hostility among others; and he was well aware of the fact that divorce might alienate a number of previously close colleagues. However, in spite of any qualms or collegiate advice to the contrary, he went through with separation and divorce from Joye. It was a break which took its toll on all concerned: one of the more notable effects for Parry was the fact that he found himself shunned by his mother, who went so far as to destroy or deface photographs of her son and a number of scrapbooks and personal effects noting his achievements throughout his life.[1] Their relationship was re-established and largely mended, however, after the birth of Marged, Gwenlyn's daughter with Ann, in 1983. The key familial relationship during the most troubled moments in the divorce was that between Gwenlyn and his younger sister Margaret, who continued to adore and idolize her brother. Gwenlyn and Ann married in 1986.

Parry's break-up and remarriage changed his life. In the most obvious sense, it brought him the experience of fatherhood again: after Marged, he and Ann had a son, Wiliam Gruffydd, in 1987 (partly named as such so that he could inherit his father's distinctive pocket watch). But it also severed relationships between him and a number of his peers and colleagues, perhaps especially those who had known Gwenlyn and Joye during the 1960s and early 1970s, when they were regarded – together – as a permanent fixture among the cultural community in Caernarfon and the Welsh-speaking society in Cardiff. Rightly or wrongly, Parry felt that he was now *persona non grata* in certain quarters: for example, he had attended Minny Street chapel in Cathays until his separation, but thereafter he felt that he had alienated himself from that congregation and could not return. Although he continued to attend religious services as part of his family duties during the 1980s, he was increasingly in retreat from the kind of organized religious practice which had been such a feature of his upbringing and cultural identity. He had also broken a kind of contract with a portion of his audience, too. That Welsh-speaking, chapel-going society had, for many years, closely and loudly identified itself as a guardian of Welsh culture – *y pethe* – and its support for literary and artistic endeavour in the language was almost unquestioning. But it could also be a highly conservative community, for whom the function of literature and art was to evangelize for a way of life removed from the worst excesses of modern permissiveness; and for whom, even in the 1980s, some of the values of contemporary, individualist living were anathema. It was a way of life, encapsulated by Gareth Miles as the 'Methodist Wales of Mari Lewis and Abel Huws',[2] in which Parry himself had been reared and which, through his divorce, he had publicly forsaken. Miles's analysis is a formidable one, noting that Parry's identity as a writer and as a man was largely typical of the 'emotional and psychological predicament of the contemporary Welsh nationalist torn between his folksy, village past and his sybaritic, suburban present':

> between the teaching of the Chapel on the perils of hard liquor and the sanctity of the family, and the alcoholic, pornographic, divorce-inclined liberalism of the eighties; between the cosy hypocrisy of the village, and the honest loneliness of the city; between hatred and love for a system which encourages alien immigration whilst boosting the Welsh language through education and the media. And in spite, or perhaps because, of all these contradictory forces, the Good Welshman still retains the essentials of Mari Lewis and Abel Huws's faith, yearning all the while for the certainties of the puritanical, unostentatious society of old.[3]

A number of years had elapsed since Parry had written for the stage; and he was now given a commission by the National Eisteddfod to write a play for production at Fishguard in 1986. True to his usual practice, he stayed very close to the events and concerns of his own life in the creation and drafting of his play; but in this case, he wrote with an unsparing and almost bewildering candour which, for some audience members, bordered on tastelessness.

Apart from its autobiographical dimension, *Panto* is also Parry's farewell to the theatre; and in that sense too, it is a play which is marked by an unredeeming harshness. It could hardly be said to glorify theatre as a medium. Instead, it presents it as a means of overexposure, of inadvertently revealing the sad and shabby truth about an individual life to a faceless, automated public. It also aggressively demystifies the business of representation, rejecting characterization and role-play as a sham to be carried out in garishly incongruous garb, which, in its grotesque excess, seems to assert that the whole enterprise is ultimately based on vanity and venality. Following on from a play (*Y Tŵr*) that could be said to indicate a mid-life crisis, *Panto* is a work which seems to issue from a kind of later life adolescence.

Panto (1986)

The play takes place on the last night of the tour of a pantomime, *Dick Whittington*, and concerns the exploits of the fading star Robert Deiniol, a well-known entertainer who plays the dame. At the beginning of the play, we see Deiniol alone in the dressing room, drinking whisky. Soon, he has fallen asleep, and, as the time for curtain up comes ever closer, the other members of the cast and backstage crew are forced to break down the door to the dressing room in order to see what has happened to him. He is drunk, and completely unfit to appear on stage. They attempt to dress him and sober him up. While most of the cast are out of the room, we learn that he has been involved in a passionate affair with Sera Rees, who plays Dic (Whittington) in the pantomime, and that she is now pregnant. He has agreed that he should reveal the truth of their affair and her pregnancy to his wife at the end of the run, and, of course, tonight is the last show of the tour. Sera precipitates the revelation by telephoning Angharad, Deiniol's wife, to tell her to come to the theatre. When she arrives, Angharad angrily confronts

Deiniol and Sera over their affair, and rebuffs Deiniol's assertion that Sera's unborn child is his. Even as Whittington's fortunes in the pantomime turn from adversity to success, Sera realizes that Deiniol will not leave Angharad, and that she will be left to raise their child on her own. The play ends with a highly-mannered conclusion which displaces the resolution of the conflict: after a song-and-dance routine in which the remaining offstage characters declare that the crock of gold at the end of the rainbow will be 'all for them', the pantomime ends and Angharad and Deiniol exit the dressing room.

Even from a bare plot outline, the autobiographical elements in *Panto* are abundantly clear. However, given what we have already observed about the relationship between Parry's life and work, this is hardly a surprise or a major shift: *Panto* is no closer to his own life than his early play *Hwyr a Bore*, for example. The main difference between those two is that *Panto* – following on from *Y Tŵr* – is far more jaded about the relationship between biography and individuality, and also has a distinct sense of catharsis or confession about it. In that respect, Parry allows the main character to be implicitly identified as himself, whereas most of his other works, including *Hwyr a Bore*, enfold the autobiographical elements into the action and express them in a less dramatically obvious way.

The confessional, cathartic nature of *Panto* need not have been such a major feature of the play – indeed, it need not have been written in the shadow of marital break-up at all. The original idea was seeded, it seems, a decade before the first production. Parry noted that the first model for Robert Deiniol – R.D. – was Ryan Davies. He had visited Ryan in his dressing room at Swansea's Grand Theatre during one of his later pantomime runs there, and had been struck by the division between the public face of the event and the private, backstage world. A number of accounts of Ryan's life have noted how he worked himself to a tragically early death, and have argued that the physical stress and exhaustion to which he submitted himself were important contributory factors. Rhydderch Jones's account of the backstage visit at the Grand is altogether more sparing, but still testifies to a split between the public and the private world of the performer:

> I went down to see the performance with Gwenlyn and to discuss a new series of 'Fo a Fe'. Bethan, [Ryan's] daughter was acting as his dresser. We were discussing the series with him in the dressing room, the tannoy was transmitting the performance from the stage. Suddenly, Ryan would vanish to perform 'his bit', return to the dressing room, only to pick up our point of discussion while Bethan helped him into his next costume. This went on quite a few times during the pantomime. Gwenlyn and myself were quite amazed.[4]

But Ryan was not the only model for Deiniol. Another contemporary incident which informed Parry's approach to the relationship between Deiniol and Sera was the revelation of an affair between the chairman of the Conservative Party, Cecil Parkinson, and his secretary, Sarah Keays. Gwenlyn even named Sera after Keays. In spite of realizing full well the charges of callousness or hypocrisy which might be levelled against him, he was incensed by Parkinson's decision to stay with his wife after Keays became pregnant with his child; and the bitterness with which he loads Deiniol's rejection and dismissal of Sera at the end of the play is at least partly due to his desire to comment on that particular incident.

These influences on the character of Deiniol notwithstanding, the extent to which the character accords with Gwenlyn himself is unmistakable. Robert Deiniol is an ageing performer, in his mid-fifties, whose identity is bound up with his vocation as a man of the theatre; but the terms of his engagement with that vocation are now changing and he is increasingly aware of the waning of his powers. He has been conducting an extramarital affair; he is a heavy drinker; and by the end of the play, he believes himself to be infertile. But, probably most tellingly of all, Deiniol's background is Parry's. He reveals it in a verbal tirade against his fellow actor Mici Tudor (who plays the Pantomime Cat, and is despised by Deiniol because of his attraction to Sera):

> DEINIOL: Look. They've all put their names up here [. . .] and no one dare write their name here in Dressing Room One if they haven't been here [. . .] no-one in this business plays games with fate! Listen – Max

Wall, Wyn Calvin, Stan Stennet, Ryan Davies . . . number one people, understand [. . .] all been in here! After all the tribulations [. . .] success! At least I made Dressing Room One, oh yes, and tonight (*He picks up a marker pen*) I can put my name on here – Robert Deiniol – a little boy from Llanbabs – bloody Hafod Ola [. . .] council houses [. . .] Gwaun Gynfi school [. . .] Higher Grade.[5]

Given the specificity of this reference, it may seem disingenuous to deny an autobiographical element to the play. But Gwenlyn – particularly in the wake of *Panto* – was keen to emphasize that, whatever the background of his characters' lives or the events of his plays, they were anything but literal representations of himself: 'some 20 per cent of me and the truth about me but . . . some 80 per cent imagination.'[6] This may be so, but the claim that the plays are substantially imaginary works does not, of course, make them any less autobiographical in essence, it merely makes their expression of the autobiographical dimension less direct. Indeed, that very indirectness – the unconscious feeling for poetic detail – might be said to be far more revealing than any consciously biographical material. In Robert Deiniol's first scene with Sera, he complains that he is finding it increasingly difficult to get work and regards himself as a spent force. There is an urgency to the sense of crisis in Deiniol's words, and to his description of his need to drink, which suggests that, even though Gwenlyn may not have directly regarded himself as such, he was intimately acquainted with their emotional force:

DEINIOL: Who'll book me next? I had to crawl to get this one. End of the road, understand. (*He walks over to the mask hanging on the wall and scrabbles around behind it. He finds a half bottle of whisky.*)
SERA: Give me that.
DEINIOL: I have to have some! (*He takes one large swig*)
SERA: Please, Deiniol.
DEINIOL: I'll be fine now. A mouthful or two to clear my head – that's all.
SERA: (*sitting sadly*) That's what controls you now, isn't it?
DEINIOL: Oh heaven, if only you understood – this (*He takes the bottle*) isn't the reason I'm like this – it's *because* I'm like this that I drink. You don't understand. The whisky's a consequence, not a reason.
SERA: You say!

DEINIOL: Look, listen. I'm a failure. I've been a failure in every bloody thing I've ever done.
SERA: You were proud earlier on that you'd made Dressing Room One.
DEINIOL: Yes. But where? This place is the arsehole of the world by now. No-one in his right mind would play here.
SERA: Everyone says you're the best Dame in the business.
DEINIOL: Dame! Fucking hell [. . .] is playing fucking Dame any measure of success? Any bloody fool can play dame. What else do I do? I ask you. Is anyone offering me anything else?[7]

Another means by which Parry deflects attention from literally autobiographical elements here is through his prevalent use of the mock-heroic as a mode of address to the narrative. The fact that Deiniol's preferred role has been that of pantomime gives his crisis a sense of the ridiculous, and suggests that Parry is deliberately undermining the dignity of a personally painful drama by subjecting it to conventions of base role-play, stereotypical narrative (bolstered by audience interaction), and grotesquely reduced and inverted notions of character (particularly feminine ones). Throughout the play, he takes every opportunity available to relate the events of Deiniol and Sera's lives to the storyline of the pantomime, even diverging from some of the traditional content of *Dick Whittington* in order to facilitate various comparisons and contrasts between the two. For example, in a confrontation scene with Sera towards the end of Act I, Deiniol expresses a deep unease about the disapproval and enmity which the betrayal of his wife will cause, and about the significant age difference between him and his lover; he is also aflame with jealousy over what he sees as inappropriate intimacy between Sera and Mici Tudor (who plays the Cat). This unsympathetic portrayal of Deiniol is played out alongside a wordless nightmare routine on the pantomime stage in which the Cat is assailed by Demons, before being saved by a Good Fairy. This has obvious, bleakly comic parallels with Deiniol's (and probably Gwenlyn's) own situation and has a reductive effect, distancing the audience from the intensity of Deiniol's personal drama and suggesting that it is, in one sense, as naive and removed from reality as its fantastical, feline parallel.

Such a comparison is greatly aided by *Panto*'s main staging device. The stage is divided throughout, and simultaneously represents the pantomime stage on one side and the theatre's backstage dressing room on the other. Just as the sudden change in Ryan Davies's energy and attention at the Grand Theatre had fascinated Parry back in the 1970s, here he creates a stage with a direct and permanent juxtaposition between public and private, onstage and offstage worlds. This kind of juxtaposition is a familiar device in modern (and even classical) theatre, but Parry's division of the play into two worlds seems to owe more to the multi-location narratives of his television work than to his theatre plays. Like *Y Tŵr*, this is a stage play that is marked by the use of devices which would not be alien to soap opera or sitcom: the layout of the stage has something of the multiple-set television studio about it, and the development of the narrative is both episodic and reliant on a kind of live montage.

Of course, *Panto* also exploits the nature of live performance to the full, and there are experiments with theatricality here that go beyond anything which Parry had attempted before. The action of *Panto* is partially located beyond the stage altogether. According to the opening stage directions, the play actually begins in the foyer, where the audience is confronted by the Stage Manager, Maldwyn, who is described as '*overseeing the foyer and greeting the audience as they arrive*'. When it becomes evident that Robert Deiniol is incapacitated, Maldwyn is summoned into the auditorium, and it is only then that the audience realizes that the figure it may have previously regarded as a member of theatre staff is in fact a member of the cast, and a fictional character from within the world of the play. The purpose of this device is to '*reveal to the audience, in due course, that the play had started the moment that they crossed the theatre's threshold, and that they, in fact, are acting in it.*'[8] This is a significant development even from *Sal*, where, although the audience's role as juror was also prescribed by the nature of the stage action, it was not called to act upon it during the show itself; and its closest counterpart as a device in Parry's work may be the revised ending for the proposed operatic version of *Tŷ ar y Tywod*, in which the action was described as spilling out into the auditorium during the climactic scene. In *Panto*, however, that overspill occurs at the very beginning, and the audience are to 'wake' to the various layers of theatricality in the play as it develops, realizing in the process that they have already been enveloped by them before even being aware of the fact.

The sense of an overspill, of an insinuation of the action directly into the audience's domain, is sustained throughout a considerable portion of the play by the presence of the mute *Dyn Llwyfan*, the 'stage hand'. Although he is only ever present within the stage action, he does not contribute actively to it but rather operates in a largely functional capacity. The stage directions stipulate from the very beginning that he is to operate *'completely mechanically'*; but nonetheless he is brought in to some of the most important and powerfully charged moments in the play, and his presence thus helps to emphasize the artificiality of the stage action throughout. For example, he is the one who precipitates the beginning of the 'proper' action of the play by breaking down the door of Deiniol's dressing room; and he is also responsible, nominally as *Mr Coediwr* ['Mr Forester'], for answering Sera's distressed plea to remove Deiniol from the stage after he has escaped the clutches of the backstage staff. Another prevalent device in the play which intrudes or 'overspills' into the audience's domain is the use of canned laughter and pre-recorded crowd responses. It too creates a sense of alienation from the action by negating its spontaneity and reducing it to the level of a mechanized reaction; and it serves to emphasize that the whole experience is very closely bounded and governed by its pre-existing conventions. It is first heard during Deiniol's brief and chaotic appearance on stage as Dame, where it supplies the expected accompaniment to the action (children's voices call out *'She's behind you!'*, as the Dame menacingly approaches Dic), but then begins to have a more direct effect on the performers, Deiniol in particular:

DEINIOL: (*Managing to kick the CAT*) Get out of my sight, you bloomin' tom!

(*The CAT is obviously injured.*)
Ha [. . .] ha [. . .] ha [. . .] ha [. . .] (*He laughs uproariously*)
I got you now didn't I [. . .] I got you!
CHILDREN: (*On tape*) Boo!
DEINIOL: (*To the audience*) Yes, but you don't know the little sneak like
I do.
CHILDREN: (*On tape*) Boo!
DEINIOL: Well boo to you too then, you horrible little buggers.[9]

The application of such pantomimic convention is accentuated
with ever greater force as the play progresses. During Act II, it begins
to be visited directly onto the characters in the backstage area,
mechanizing their actions, and disrupting the play's basic sense
of realism. This is first seen when Sera and Elin taunt Maldwyn
about his supposed sexual indiscretions on tour. As they do so,
they break into a series of sudden and quite incongruous dance
steps:

ELIN: He had a go at me in the back of the van between Llanidloes and
Llangurig.
MALDWYN: I did no such fucking thing!
SERA: 'Attempted rape of wardrobe mistress in Pantechnicon.'
ELIN: And he offered me money.
SERA: 'Bribery and corruption with Dic!'
(*Suddenly SERA performs two or three quick dance moves.*)
ELIN: 'Encouraging soliciting!'
(*ELIN also performs two or three dance moves.*)

From this point on in the play, the realistic human drama between
Deiniol, Sera, Angharad and the rest of the cast is increasingly
undermined by theatrical stylization until, finally, any sense of
independent volition or willed action on their part is circumscribed
by artifice. All the characters are rendered robotic. Angharad's
entry into the scene, for example, ought to signal the dramatic high
point of the play, but instead it accelerates the use of devices which
serve to deaden the action and reduce it to the level of theatrical
routine. As she, Deiniol and Sera argue in the dressing room, the

taped effect of the young pantomime audience breaks into their nominally private conversation:

> ANGHARAD: He chooses the same model every year, except that the 'reg number' is a little newer than the one he's got.
> DEINIOL: That's completely untrue.
> ANGHARAD: Oh no it isn't.
> DEINIOL: Oh yes it is.
> CHILDREN: (*on tape*) Oh no it isn't.
> DEINIOL: Oh yes it is.[10]

Furthermore, as their conflict intensifies, they spontaneously – '*as is the rule in pantomime, albeit without accompaniment*'[11] – break into song: it is a moment which undermines the primacy and pain of their dramatic situation (one which must have been directly experienced by Parry himself) and aggressively dehumanizes them. And the same device is visited upon the entire cast a few moments later, as they are formally and mechanically costumed for the finale of the show which, somewhat unexpectedly but not inconsistently, takes place in the dressing room rather than on the stage. Sera is excised from the finale and driven out, and the remaining cast join in a song which parrots their dreams and expectations for the future: 'There's treasure at the end of the rainbow./ We'll have the lot,/ Pure gold in the pot./ That's our reward.'[12] As they begin to sing, the Stage Hand slides the divide between the dressing room and the pantomime stage across so that the nominally private backstage now occupies three-quarters of the total area. That private domain, which denoted the seat of the individual psyche at the beginning of the play, has been totally absorbed into the fiction, and any sense of personal volition on the part of the characters has been ceded to the inherent dramaturgy of their role. It is a Pirandellian conceit played out in reverse.

Panto comes to an end, then, on a distinctly downbeat note. But this is not the play's most characteristic feature. Its deadening and defeatist conclusion is no match for the moments of unrestrainable passion and energy which transcend and explode the confines of the stage. For example, when Deiniol (who is enraged at his exclusion from the pantomime, the other actors having attempted to improvise the show without the Dame), breaks out from his dressing room and bursts onto the stage, he exerts a rather joyously liberating force which is significant in itself. Despite the chaos which he creates by departing from the script and assaulting his fellow actor Mici Tudor, he is momentarily free of the constraints (many of them self-imposed) which have impeded the full expression of his libidinous energy. He is juxtaposed against the anxious Maldwyn, the Stage Manager, who sits slumped in a chair in the dressing room, despairing of his failure to contain the situation and to repress the release of such unseemly passions. This, it seems, is the play's authentic voice, and the climactic reduction of the action to a series of robotic routines at the end feels rather too convenient to be true. Like the murder of the German soldier back in *Y Ddraenen Fach*, it is merely a means of bringing the action to a close, and it does not dispense with the fundamental energy which has been released in the process of conceiving and enacting the play. Parry may well have felt the same way, as he licensed a moment of almost defiant inconclusion at the very end of the play:

> ANGHARAD: (*to Deiniol*) Come on. We'll go home. Everything will be fine now, you'll see. (*Deiniol and Angharad turn to leave through the door. But the voice of a young child is heard [ideally, this should reverberate through the auditorium]*)
> CHILD: Oh, no it won't [. . .] Oh, no it won't [. . .] Oh, no it won't [. . .] Oh, no it won't [. . .] (*The voice gradually fades*)[13]

It is a conclusion which is not so much tragic as sullen. Like so much of the play, it lacks a sense of dignity, something which had been so evident in his work up until this point. Even where his characters were left in a pitiable state, as in *Y Ffin*, the form and theatrical resonance of his work suggested an intensity of vision which was never less than honest. In *Panto*, however, for all the highly personal material in the play, his theatricality is imbued with a rather tired cynicism which occasionally verges on the poisonous.[14] The grotesque defacing of femininity in the play, for example, is a world away from the reverential curiosity which characterized his treatment of female figures in the trilogy. The Dummy of *Tŷ ar y Tywod* is replaced by the Dame of *Panto*; and, though both involve a problematic objectification of the female, the Dummy at least has the effect of implying the elevating, idealistic nature of the spectacle. In *Panto*, the Dame is grossly reductive, and associated with an ironically perverse and grotesque ardour. When Deiniol puts on the costume at the beginning of the play, he is transformed into a bizarre combination of lothario, abusive older woman and (drunken) infant:

> DEINIOL: Gi' 's a kiss (*He fumbles for her*)
> SERA: Stop your grabbing and put this on your head. (*She puts a wig on his head*)
> DEINIOL: (*seizing her by the waist, and pulling her tight to him*) A little one!
> SERA: Why didn't you meet me, then, like you promised?
> DEINIOL: Kiss!
> SERA: You silly baby! (*She yields to him and nears his lips, but is overcome by his whisky-laden breath*) Oh my God – you smell like a brewery![15]

The role of Dame is passed on from Deiniol to Maldwyn in Act II, whereupon he performs an almost Pentheus-like switch from anxious controller of the action to its chief clown. He is 'infected' by the energy of the role and becomes increasingly relaxed, self-congratulatory and intimate with Sera. But the most telling, and cruellest, manifestation of the Dame is Angharad, who affects the dramatic action and the theatrical presentation at almost every level and drags the play, as if kicking and screaming, to a hasty conclusion. Her most important function is to effectively 'castrate' Deiniol by undermining his self-confidence and his image of himself as a man. She suggests to him that her supposed infertility was a lie which she perpetuated in order to spare him from pain. While Deiniol listens on, she tells Sera that 'This one's only ever fired blanks – don't you understand [. . .] a water pistol! . . . But I had all the tests . . . and my tubes were as clear as the Mersey Tunnel on Christmas Day'.[16] This, of course, strongly implies that Sera's baby has been fathered by somebody else, a suggestion which, in spite of Sera's previous protestations to the contrary, Angharad hammers home: 'you'll never be sure', she tells Deiniol; 'A man only *believes*, but a woman *knows*!'[17] Deiniol is rendered babbling and inarticulate, and, having had his sense of his potency as a male undermined, he gradually resigns himself to the idea that his passion for Sera is insubstantial and unreal.

It had been Parry's original intention to give Sera Rees the last word in the play. Standing alone on the diminished and darkened pantomime stage, she was to have provided a wearily sobering epitaph to the whole charade: 'London's streets are paved with concrete, just like every other.'[18] However, as had been the case with *Saer Doliau*, he allowed the final moment of the play to be reworked in rehearsal and to be altered by the suggestion of the cast; and the final moment was instead given over to Deiniol and Angharad, and to the disembodied voice of a child. It is altogether a more fitting climax, given that the most prevalent device during the second half of Act II had been the mechanization of the action, and given that, throughout his career, the implicit conversation between child and adult had been one of the mainstays of his dramatic vision.

Presenting *Panto* in public was evidently something of an ordeal for Parry. The night before the opening performance by Theatr Whare Teg at the Fishguard Eisteddfod, he was literally sick with nervous trepidation, knowing that the reaction to the play would be intense. But, as noted by the actress Sue Roderick – who played Angharad – he 'had to write the play in order to get the experience out of his system';[19] and he must have been gratified by the audience's enthusiastic response on the night.[20] However, in her review of the production in *Y Cymro*, Eleri Rogers noted that the play itself came dangerously close to self-indulgence in its foregrounding of the 'mindless but endearing selfishness' of the main character. Although she praised the production for its effective staging and for the performances of the cast (especially John Ogwen in the role of Robert Deiniol), she criticized it for its callousness in riding roughshod over the feelings of those who were implicated in Parry's autobiographical *confessio* without necessarily giving their consent:

> When a personal catharsis gives rise to literature which is exciting and enriches its audience's experience – fine. Fine for the writer himself, but the extent to which one can justify profiting from the experiences of those who were an intrinsic part of the situation is another matter.[21]

'Everything will be fine now, you'll see': Later Life

After *Panto*, Parry wrote no more stage plays. He channelled his creative energies into his television work and, increasingly, into film. It is tempting to suggest that, after *Panto*, his appetite for theatre was spent, and that he had gone as far as he could. In a simpler and more immediate sense, however, his work for television and film gave him a means to earn a living, whereas theatre (as ever) could not. The 'hackwork' at the BBC went on, most notably with *Hafod Henri*, a television sitcom written alongside Rhydderch Jones, which attempted to recreate the success of *Fo a Fe* (which was still widely regarded as the most successful Welsh sitcom to that date). *Hafod Henri* was set in a country hotel run by a retired Army officer, Henri Maelor, who was determined to create a sense of luxury at his establishment by appealing to an old, if not lost, Welsh aristocratic tradition and by creating indigenous gourmet cuisine. The nobility of this cause was constantly hampered, however, by the distinctly brusque attitudes of his staff, whose scheming practicality constantly brought Maelor's fanciful ideas and plans back down to earth: there was more than a hint of Wil Napoleon and Mons about a number of them. It was a relatively popular series during its comparatively brief span, but the idiosyncrasies of the writing and characterization never really melded into a coherent whole and it has dated badly over the years.

Like *Fo a Fe*, it was truncated by the death of a key collaborator. Rhydderch Jones died on 4 November 1987, a date which prompted Gwenlyn to shroud his pain in a thoroughly appropriate wry humour: 'A shame that he couldn't have waited until the 5th and gone out with a bang.'[1] His relationship with Rhydderch had been of great importance throughout his life, and many of those close to him have suggested that Gwenlyn never really recovered from the loss. They had never compromised in their friendship, and were 'closer than two brothers', because, according to Gwenlyn, 'two brothers can't tell the truth to each other . . . but two very, very close friends can sometimes say cruel things to each other for the benefit of each other.' And Rhydderch – 'a very Puritanical man in his way . . . You'd be surprised'[2] – had been intensely, cruelly honest with Parry on many occasions, particularly at the time of his divorce. But his final analysis of him was of a deep loyalty, sympathy and love: Rhydderch, 'more than anyone else, exerted an influence not only on my work but also on my personality, my way of life, my attitude towards life, my sense of humour, . . . to the point at which I would say that I became a part of him'.[3]

Work continued: and in the later 1980s, the most important projects with which Parry was most closely associated were in the field of film. This was a period in which funding for major features through co-production via the auspices of the BBC in Wales and S4C had made the creation of feature films and larger-scale television dramas far more achievable and affordable than they had been before, and Parry took full advantage of those opportunities. The most notable film projects which came his way included *I Fro Breuddwydion/A Penny for your Dreams*, a fantasy biopic about the Welsh film pioneer William Haggar, which he scripted alongside director Ken Howard; and *Un Nos Ola Leuad* [known in English as 'One full moon'], adapted from Caradog Pritchard's famous novel with the director Endaf Emlyn.

I Fro Breuddwydion was produced 'back-to-back' in Welsh and English, as was the custom for the bigger budget co-productions which were in vogue at the time. It was a relatively conventional but quite complex screenplay which wove together a historical story with a contemporary analogy. It was first broadcast over Christmas in 1987 and was well received, going on to win the Spirit of the Festival Award at the Celtic Film Festival in 1988. The fact that it was a film about film gave it a link to Parry's recent *Panto*, a theatre play about theatre; and, as in that play, there was a liberal use of narrative devices which drew attention to the medium through which the story was being presented to its audience. These were used to describe the experience of falling in love with film (both in the present and in Haggar's time) and also to make the transitional links between the two time periods. Unlike *Panto*, however, *I Fro Breuddwydion* was nowhere near as burdened with Gwenlyn's own apprehensions and fears: in spite of the tribulations of Haggar's life and career, this was a relatively upbeat story. But the same certainly could not be said about Parry's final film project, the adaptation of Caradog Pritchard's *Un Nos Ola Leuad*.

As noted already, the novel had influenced Gwenlyn greatly, even before it was published in 1961; more importantly, it was a landmark work in terms of its conflation of childish innocence, sex, madness and the landscape of industrial north Wales, and was a breakthrough in terms of furthering and popularizing literary modernism in Welsh. It translated the kind of experience which had been central to Gwenlyn's own childhood into elaborate fiction; and could be said to have helped to create the imaginary terrain in which Gwenlyn located a number of his own characters, such as Bili Puw in *Poen yn y Bol* and the Man of the House in *Tŷ ar y Tywod* (the punchline in the story of Dic Fflat in *Y Tŵr* is also taken from Pritchard's radio draft of *Un Nos Ola Leuad*).

It was a kind of return to the milieu and storyline with which he was most at home. His outline version of the film set the action in both the present day and in the years 1916–18, and, in keeping with the novel, portrayed a rather distressed and confused old man (the Narrator) returning to the village of his birth in order to seek out some of the places which had been central to his life some sixty years previously. Parry's take on the material was rather gentle and tenderly comic, akin to Pritchard's own radio script, and was driven by its dialogue rather than its visual imagery (in many ways, it bore a marked resemblance to *Gwenoliaid* and *Lliwiau*, the last two film scripts by Rhydderch Jones). This approach put him at odds with the vision of the director, Endaf Emlyn, whose preferred interpretation was considerably more stark and sparing;

and the difference between the two men's working scripts tells us a good deal about the extent to which Gwenlyn's basic approach was more suited to theatre than film. Gwenlyn's early drafts insisted on the coexistence of the spoken word and the visual image, with a number of the shots outlined in the screenplay also being described verbally by the Narrator; Emlyn wanted to dispense with the Narrator figure altogether and let the pictures tell their own, often ambiguous, story. The two of them came to some kind of accommodation in their final draft; but the process was a confirmation, and a true test, of the description which Gwenlyn had given a few years before of writing for film as collective experience rather than the fulfilment of an individual vision:

> I think that film really is not the author's work, it's basically a co-op, and it's a director's medium; and if the author can't sort of sit back sometimes and say, 'well, that's a great idea', if they can't each work with each other, I feel, having worked in that medium, it can be a flop. The film, to me, is group work.[4]

This principle had served him well enough during the filming and production of *Grand Slam*, but the experience of having to adapt a vision which was so close to his heart was not a pleasurable one. In that sense, times had changed quite considerably for Parry. Sion Eirian notes that, by the end of the 1980s, he was well aware of the fact that time and developments in media production were moving ahead without him; the kind of 'court' over which he and Rhydderch had presided at the BBC was very largely a thing of the past. Indeed, it is debatable, particularly after Jones's death, and as Parry neared retirement from the BBC, to what extent his heart was still in the work (for example, his occasional scripts for Eirian's 1960s-based series *Mwy na Phapur Newydd* had to be edited somewhat indulgently in order to remove anachronistic details). The television industry was changing, and production principles were being adjusted and reshaped in order to conform to the needs of increasing budgetary and formulaic constraints. Having been invited to attend a three-day seminar by the American script guru Robert McKee in 1989, Parry and Eirian were both struck by the ranks of young writers and editors from S4C, avidly taking notes, and could sense that a major change was in the air: they retired to the Woodville Arms, where Gwenlyn spent the rest of the afternoon scribbling notes towards *Un Nos Ola Leuad*.[5]

What this kind of change would have meant for any future phase of his career beyond *Un Nos Ola Leuad* and outside the BBC is, of course, conjectural. Gwenlyn fell ill in the spring of 1991, and was diagnosed with cancer. Treatment for the condition was harsh, and proved ineffective. He remained at home in Hafod Olau, Pencisely Road during the summer months, visited regularly by his old friends, but seldom venturing out. He was admitted to the Holme Towers Hospice in Penarth on 3 October. On that first night in Penarth, he looked out over the Bristol Channel at the islands of Flatholm and Steepholm, and was told of an old tradition that the body of Thomas à Becket had been secretly buried on Flatholm, the smaller of the two. The lighthouse on Flatholm shone in the night; and when his long-time colleague Meic Povey came to see him there, he was told that this view was peculiarly significant for Gwenlyn, giving him a 'sense of strength and succour, and [making] him feel that, perhaps, someone was 'calling' him'.[6] Parry wrote a poem recounting this experience, which was published in the journal *Taliesin* in 1992:

BORE BACH	[EARLY MORNING
Dwy ynys draw	Two islands away
Yn y niwl –	In the mist –
Un fel toes	One like dough
Yn ei lawn dwf,	Risen to the full,
A'r llall yn	The other
Fflat fel crempog.	Flat as a pancake.
Maent yn dweud	They say
Fod Beckett yn	That Beckett
Gorwedd yn dawel	Lies peacefully
Yng Nghaergaint.	In Canterbury.
Ai dyna pam	Is that why
Mae'r fach yn wincian?	The little one is winking?][7]

Ann Beynon noted that, towards the end of his life, he had expressed a sense of completeness and satisfaction, saying that he was content with what he had achieved:[8] the storm which had, latterly, raged through a character like Robert Deiniol in *Panto*, was stilled. He died in the early morning of 5 November 1991. Harri Pritchard Jones recalls a similar sense of calm towards the end:

> As he sickened and faced death, Gwenlyn kept considering the old questions, without expecting a definite answer. But the foul old shadows departed and he died in peace. He had contributed greatly to our own growth away from superstition and old irrational fears, to face the real challenge of life and death.[9]

His funeral was held at Bethel chapel in Penygroes on 9 November, and he was buried at Macpela cemetery. The inscription on his gravestone indicates his final, abiding description of himself: 'Dramatist'.

His obituary in *The Independent* was penned by his friend and long-time colleague John Hefin. Gwenlyn, he said, 'was one of the great storytellers. Timing and exaggeration were his God-given gifts. He was the complete natural master of his listeners' emotions.'[10] Elan Closs Stephens, in a tribute in *Golwg*, described him as 'the least realistic of Welsh playwrights, who gave us the capacity to be truly realistic in terms of dialogue and emotion.'[11] And, in a more recent tribute, Meic Povey summed up his contribution to the bolstering of drama as a medium in contemporary Wales as follows:

> It was Gwenlyn who, as a stage playwright, was chiefly responsible for revolutionising Welsh language theatre during the 1960s and 1970s, entrancing and encouraging many of us to follow in his footsteps. He was also a pioneer in the field of television; personally, I would claim that he deserves to be called 'the father of modern Welsh language television drama'. No-one wrote soap operas, in the true sense of the word, until he took up the craft and showed the way ahead for everyone else. It is only today, perhaps, that we can fully appreciate his influence.[12]

One of the most interesting remarks made at the time of Gwenlyn's death, however, were recalled by Harri Pritchard Jones in his own tribute in *Taliesin*. During a conversation between them, which had taken place at the time of Gwenlyn's retirement from the BBC in 1988, he had asserted that, in future, he would stop 'navel-gazing all the time, and trying to prove something'; he would be 'less allegorical, more imaginative – and definitely less moralistic. There'll be less rummaging about in that old cellar [. . .] more romance [. . .] less cynicism.'[13] It is a series of observations which suggest that, at that time, he had put his theatrical writing behind him, and had dispensed with the anxieties which, whether consciously bidden or not, had issued from it throughout his career as a writer.

His loss was felt particularly acutely by those who had derived so much pleasure from the joviality of his company over the years, and by those who had remained loyal friends. But his death was also dwelt upon in a curious way. He became one of those figures who was routinely described as 'late' for years after his demise (in a way which is still, on occasion, the case for his colleague Ryan Davies). At fifty-nine, he was not a particularly young man, nor could he be said to be at the height of his creative powers; but it may be explicable by the fact that he had been a key figure in the zeitgeist of the theatre and television in Wales during the majority of his career, and the fact that he had been such extraordinarily good company to so many. He was, as one rather satirical commentator put it in 1987 (after *Private Eye*) 'our GLP (Greatest National/ Welsh/ Playwright/ of the Century)',[14] and conformed to the ebullient image of the inveterate theatre man. Others pointed to the uncanny aspects of his death, and to instances which suggested the kind of message from beyond which had so stirred him and to which he had obliquely referred in some of his plays: there was a kind of irony to the fact that he died on Guy Fawkes Night, four years and a day after Rhydderch Jones, and on the very date which he had wryly recommended as the proper moment for his great friend and co-writer's demise. But it was perhaps also the kind of fiction which he created in his theatre which gave a special poignancy to his own mortality. His was a drama which was concerned with the plight of the individual thrown into being, whose own inner existence was felt to be deeply at odds with the world around them, but whose comprehension of that world had been richly furnished by the language given to them, which they then used to express their sense of loss and alienation. This particular form reached its highpoint with *Y Tŵr*, which, in addition, encapsulated a point of view which balanced detail in observing the facts of people's lives with a kind of assumed immortality in terms of its narrative agency. The Tower is beyond mortality; and, though he had turned his back on the kind of dramatic vision that he had created in the play which takes its name, it lives on in his reputation as the most significant Welsh playwright of his age.

Postscript

A work which remained unfinished at the time of Parry's death provides a kind of postscript to his life. It is a film script, provisionally entitled *Vera Lynn a 'Nhad* ['Vera Lynn and my father'], and portrays the growing years of a young boy whose father had left for the war, and whose relationship with his mother consequently became suffused with his own fantasies about being the man of the house. It brought Gwenlyn back to his childhood once again, and to his experiences at home between the ages of seven and thirteen. It was these events which, one way or another, had been at the centre of so much of his drama, and which had helped to form that combination of fantastical freedom and anxious constraint which had typified such a great deal of his stage imagery.[1]

We now witness a scene at Bangor station about a month later. It is a cold, wet morning and Ifan, Marged and Now are sheltering in a corner of the platform. Only a handful of people are there expecting the 'Mail' from Holyhead. This is the day of Ifan's departure for the war, but there is little conversation between him and his wife. Indeed, Marged is quite curt with her husband and scolds him for one thing and another. ['You should be in the quarry like everyone else.' He apologizes: 'I have to go – for the sake of this boy'.]

Now looks rather sad, but suddenly, in a flash of fantasy, Bangor station changes completely. It is now full of banners and posters saying 'Good Luck Ifan', 'We're Proud of You Ifan', 'Give Hitler a Hiding Ifan'. Even the Deiniolen Band is there to celebrate his 'embarkation'. By now his mother is the living image of Vera Lynn and is extremely smart in uniform. She sings to Ifan (who is now sitting and looking out of the train window) 'We'll meet again – don't know where, don't know when [. . .]' etc. The train's whistle shatters Now's dreams. His father is still looking out at him and his mother through the train window, but it is just a cold, silent, wet and empty platform around them now.

As the train slowly pulls away from the platform, Ifan says to Now: 'Look after your mother until I come home, my boy.' [He gives him the key to the snooker cue case: 'Practise while I'm away – we'll have a hell of a game when I get back.']

Throughout the war, Now takes his father's place more and more, and as he grows his fantasies decrease and give way to the reality of his growing pains.

When his father returns home at the end of the war, he is a stranger to Now and a kind of obstruction between him and his mother (if not a cause of jealousy).

Seeing his father fondling his mother's bottom in the small hours after he returned unannounced was quite a shock to him. ['You'd better go to your bed, my son'.]

When his mother tells him to go to his bedroom, he sits alone by his gramophone and plays a record. [He hears the sound of laughter, running up the stairs and his mother's door banging shut.] When he hears Vera Lynn singing '– and Jimmy will go to sleep, in his own little room again' – he realizes that he is Jimmy.

A kind of competitiveness grows between him and his father [. . .], but he is put neatly and firmly in his place – because Ifan is now a very different man after having been away [. . .] – and Marged now knows her place. Now suddenly realizes that he no longer needs to romanticize about his father any more. His admiration for him grows – but Now has always been a dreamer, and he cannot stop seeing himself at some remote front line with Vera Lynn singing to him: 'My Son, My Son, My Only Pride and Joy'.

But she isn't Vera Lynn of course. And it isn't his mother in the uniform either but – Sheila May [his older cousin] [. . .] and the skirt of her uniform is about an inch shorter than Vera Lynn's ever was.

Notes

Introduction

1   Jean Duvignaud, 'The theatre in society: society in theatre', in E. Burns and T. Burns (eds), *The Sociology of Literature and Drama* (Harmondsworth: Penguin Education, 1973), p. 85.

I

1   National Library of Wales [NLW], Gwenlyn Parry Papers [GPP] 5/8. Handwritten biographical notes.
2   NLW, GPP 5/5. Transcript of interview with John S. Roberts.
3   'Gwenlyn Parry', in Eleri Hopcyn (ed.), *Dylanwadau* (Llandysul: Gomer, 1995), p. 43.
4   Gwenlyn Parry, 'Gwenlyn Parry yn deud ei stori', *Antur*, 15, 5 (May 1979), 11.
5   Ibid.
6   NLW, GPP 5/8.
7   NLW, GPP 5/5.
8   Hopcyn (ed.), 'Gwenlyn Parry', p. 38.
9   Ibid.
10 Margaret Parry, interviewed for the tribute television broadcast *Cofio Gwenlyn* (John Hefin (dir.): Cambrensis, 2001).
11 Hopcyn (ed.), 'Gwenlyn Parry', p. 44.
12 NLW, GPP 5/5.
13 Ibid.
14 Hopcyn (ed.), 'Gwenlyn Parry', p. 44.
15 Ibid., p. 41.
16 NLW, GPP 5/5. He refers to Thomas Williams ('Tom Nefyn'; 1895–1958), minister and evangelist; and E. Tegla Davies (1880–1967), minister and influential writer.
17 Hopcyn (ed.), 'Gwenlyn Parry', p. 46.

[18] NLW, GPP 5/5.

[19] Hopcyn (ed.), 'Gwenlyn Parry', p. 44.

[20] Ibid.

[21] Ann Beynon relates how Gwenlyn had been shown how to embalm corpses during his period of National Service; and how his story about the embalming of Lebanese pilots greatly intrigued his London friend John Daniel Jones. When he died, at a tragically early age, he made it a rather unexpected condition of his will that Gwenlyn should view his body before burial. John Dan had had himself embalmed according to the same procedure that Gwenlyn described in his story. Ann Beynon, interview, 27 August 2011.

[22] Hopcyn (ed.). 'Gwenlyn Parry', p. 44.

[23] Ibid., p. 45.

[24] Ibid., p. 47.

[25] Ibid., p. 50. The final line is a quotation from T. H. Parry-Williams's poem *Hon*; see *Ugain o Gerddi* (Aberystwyth: Gwasg Aberystwyth, 1949), pp. 12–13. The word *'hon'* is difficult to translate succinctly in this context. Literally, it is the feminine form of the demonstrative pronoun meaning 'this one', and is rendered as such in the English translation found in R. Gerallt Jones (ed.), *Poetry of Wales 1930–1970* (Llandysul: Gomer, 1974), p. 61. Joseph P. Clancy, in a more colloquial style, translates the title as 'This Spot'. See Joseph P. Clancy, *Twentieth-Century Welsh Poems* (Llandysul: Gomer Press, 1982), pp. 71–2.

2

[1] William Thomas and Thomas Mons Bevan: see 'Gwenlyn Parry', in Eleri Hopcyn (ed.), *Dylanwadau* (Llandysul: Gomer, 1995), p. 51. Gwenlyn can be heard recounting his stories about the two in the radio broadcast of *Dylanwadau*, BBC Radio Cymru, first broadcast 13 September 1989. For a tribute to Mons, see John Roberts Williams, 'Mons', *Taliesin* (March 1988), 44.

[2] National Library of Wales [NLW], Gwenlyn Parry Papers [GPP] 5/8. Handwritten biographical notes.

[3] Dates in brackets after the titles of Parry's plays indicate their earliest known date of completion and presentation, either as scripts submitted for Eisteddfod competitions or for stage production.

[4] Gwenlyn Parry, 'Y Ddraenen Fach', *Tair Drama Fer* (Denbigh: Gwasg Gee, 1965), p. 14.

[5] Ibid., p. 15.

6   The *noson lawen* (literally 'merry evening') is a form of variety concert. In its original form, one of its central elements was an impromptu poetic competition; but latterly it has been used as a term to describe any kind of evening's entertainment which might include singing, dancing, recitation, stand-up comedy and dramatic sketches.

7   Emyr Humphreys, 'Drama wreiddiol fer', in Stephen J. Williams (ed.), *Cyfansoddiadau a Beirniadaethau Eisteddfod Genedlaethol Frenhinol Cymru Llanelli a'r Cylch 1962* (Llandysul: Gomer on behalf of the Court of the National Eisteddfod, 1962), p. 212.

8   J. Ellis Williams, 'Drama wreiddiol fer', in William Morris (ed.), *Cyfansoddiadau a Beirniadaethau Eisteddfod Genedlaethol Frenhinol Cymru Llandudno a'r Cylch 1963* (Llandysul: Gomer on behalf of the Court of the National Eisteddfod, 1963), p. 174.

9   See Huw Roberts, 'Nes na'r hanesydd?', *Cyntedd* (Fishguard National Eisteddfod edn, 1986), p. 4.

10   See NLW, GPP 5/6

11   Gwenlyn Parry, 'Poen yn y Bol', *Tair Drama Fer* (Denbigh: Gwasg Gee, 1965), p. 57.

12   Ibid., p. 58 (with appropriate alterations). For the letter from the Office of the Lord Chamberlain, see NLW, GPP 7/1. Letter [to 'Miss Gwenlyn Parry'], dated 9 March 1964. The 'uncensored' version was adopted for the broadcast version of the play, under the title 'Un Dau Tri', on BBC television, 7 March 1972.

13   Parry, 'Poen yn y Bol', p. 58.

14   See Slavoj Žižek, *The Pervert's Guide to the Cinema* (Sophie Fiennes (dir.): Amoeba Film, 2006).

15   Parry, 'Poen yn y Bol', p. 43.

16   Gareth Miles, 'Bardd y *di-sens*', *Barn* (June 2008), 61. For a reliable account of the events, see Dafydd Glyn Jones, 'Peth o'r gwir am lwyth o gelwydd', *Barn* (March 2009), 47–51; and Rhiannon Parry, 'O lygad y ffynnon', *Barn* (March 2009), 51–4. The students involved in *Y Ffynnon* were John Roberts, Iorwerth Roberts, Rhiannon Price, Dafydd Glyn Jones from Bangor and Geraint Jones from University College Wales, Aberystwyth. The text of *Y Ffynnon* was published in *Taliesin* in July 1986. See 'Taliesin', ' "Y Ffynnon" a chyflwyniad', *Taliesin*, 56 (July 1986), 38–48.

17   D. R. Davies, 'Festival a "must" for the future', *Western Mail* (11 April 1964), 4. For the previously offending article, see 'A rural extravaganza', *Western Mail* (West edition: 9 April 1964), 9.

18   D. Jacob Davies, 'Angen cefnogi'r bechgyn a'r merched brwd', *Y Cymro* (16 April 1964), 12–13.

19   Miles, 'Bardd y *di-sens*', 61.

20 Gwenlyn Parry, 'Hwyr a Bore', *Tair Drama Fer* (Denbigh: Gwasg Gee, 1965), p. 43.

21 Ibid., p. 38.

22 Ibid., p. 49.

3

1 See William R. Lewis, 'Huw Lloyd Edwards: comedïwr, moesolwr a bardd', *Taliesin*, 61 (March 1988), 46–58.

2 Joye Evans Parry, interviewed in *Cofio Gwenlyn* (John Hefin (dir.), 2001).

3 Joye Evans Parry, interviewed for BBC website *http://www.bbc.co.uk/cymru/gwenlyn/dramodydd/atgofion_jp.shtml* (accessed 18 November 2012).

4 'Gwenlyn Parry', in Eleri Hopcyn (ed.), *Dylanwadau* (Llandysul: Gomer, 1995), p. 55.

5 National Library of Wales [NLW], Gwenlyn Parry Papers [GPP] 5/5.

6 Hopcyn (ed.), 'Gwenlyn Parry', p. 54.

7 Ibid.

8 NLW, GPP 5/5.

9 Ibid.

10 It should also be remembered that the renowned Welsh philosopher J. R. Jones produced a small but seriously challenging publication on the same theme about a year after *Honest to God*: entitled *Yr Argyfwng Gwacter Ystyr* ['The crisis of meaninglessness'], it also explored Tillich's ideas and approaches to contemporary anxieties within Christian belief. The title of Jones's work became a watchword for the crises of modernist literature in Welsh, particularly in relation to the Absurd. See J. R. Jones, *Yr Argyfwng Gwacter Ystyr* (Llandybïe: Llyfrau'r Dryw, 1964).

11 NLW, GPP 5/5.

12 Ibid.

13 Ibid.

14 John A. T. Robinson, *Honest to God* (London: SCM Press, 1963), p. 28.

15 Gwenlyn Parry, *Saer Doliau* (Llandybïe; Llyfrau'r Dryw: 1966), p. 11.

16 Ibid., p. 18.

17 Aneirin Talfan Davies, preface to Parry, *Saer Doliau*, p. 7.

18 Parry, *Saer Doliau*, p. 15.

19 This is more pronounced in the Welsh text, where the order of syntax is reversed: 'Dim. Dw i'n gwneud dim. Edrych ydw i.' Ibid.

20 'Drama gynhyrfus ar daith', *Baner ac Amserau Cymru* (7 April 1966), 1.

21 Dewi Z. Phillips, *Dramâu Gwenlyn Parry* (2nd edn; Caernarfon: Gwasg Pantycelyn, 1995), p. 44.

22 Eleanor Dwyryd, 'Noson gyntaf "Saer Doliau"', *Baner ac Amserau Cymru* (28 April 1966), 2.

23 'Gwledd o ddramau yn Aberafan', *Baner ac Amserau Cymru* (28 July 1966), 7.

24 'Ledled Cymru', *Baner ac Amserau Cymru* (28 April 1966), 4. Other reviewers echoed this enthusiasm. Harri Pritchard Jones, writing a few weeks later, noted that the 'pity in the play is that the Saer's response to the Apprentice and the Visitor is typified by hatred and illogical fear. We see a lack both of sympathy and the desire to know in the Apprentice's attitude to the Saer, in contrast to his uncomfortable obedience to the Visitor.' See Harri Pritchard Jones, 'Saer Doliau', *Baner ac Amserau Cymru* (19 May 1966), 5.

25 J. S. Williams, 'Saer Doliau (Gwenlyn Parry)', *Baner ac Amserau Cymru* (6 October 1966), 4.

26 'Dyddiadur Daniel', *Baner ac Amserau Cymru* (11 August 1966), 4.

27 NLW, GPP 7/1. Gwilym R. Tilsley, letter to Gwenlyn Parry, dated 20 April 1966: Tilsley's letter refers to Gwilym R. Jones, poet, novelist and editor; Mathonwy Hughes, literary figure and journalist; and Kate Roberts, novelist.

28 'Aprad', 'Saer Cyboliau', *Barn* (November 1966), 13.

29 'Radio a theledu', *Baner ac Amserau Cymru* (13 October 1966), 4. *Disgwyl Cwmni* had been broadcast on BBC television on Sunday afternoon, 9 October 1966.

30 Joye Evans Parry, interview, 26 August 2011. In this regard, it is also worth quoting Joye Evans Parry's assessment of this event during an interview for the television tribute programme *Cofio Gwenlyn* in 2001: 'As a young man, he was a humble man; he had this gift, and he accepted it, but he didn't think that he had anything truly excellent.' See *Cofio Gwenlyn* (Hefin (dir.), 2001).

4

1 Gwenlyn Parry, introduction to *Tŷ ar y Tywod* (Llandybïe: Christopher Davies, 1969), p. 9.

2 John Rowlands, 'Saer Doliau a'r theatr ddwl', *Y Traethodydd* (October 1968), 159.

3 Ibid., 161.

4 Parry, introduction to *Tŷ ar y Tywod*, p. 9.

5   Gwenlyn Parry, 'Y busnes sgrifennu 'ma', *Llwyfan*, 2 (spring 1969), 15.
6   Parry, introduction to *Tŷ ar y Tywod*, p. 9.
7   Dafydd Glyn Jones, 'Theatr, drama a llenyddiaeth', *Baner ac Amserau Cymru* (15 August 1968), 8.
8   Ibid.
9   National Library of Wales [NLW], Gwenlyn Parry Papers [GPP] 1/2. '*Tŷ ar y Tywod*: some thoughts on the play'.
10 Ibid.
11 NLW, GPP 7/1. Aneirin Talfan Davies, memo dated 21 May 1968.
12 NLW, GPP 1/2. '*Tŷ ar y Tywod*: some thoughts on the play'.
13 Parry, *Tŷ ar y Tywod*, p. 13.
14 Ibid., p. 25.
15 Ibid., p. 14.
16 Ibid., p. 21.
17 It is worth noting that, in an earlier draft of the play, there was another female figure who intervened in the action: a middle-aged woman with a voice described as being 'soft [and] hypnotic like a psychiatrist', but who was strikingly hard in appearance upon entry into the shack, looking like 'a Prison Warder in her Sunday clothes'. See NLW, GPP 1/2.
18 Parry, *Tŷ ar y Tywod*, p. 26.
19 Ibid., p. 39.
20 Ibid.
21 Ibid., p. 28.
22 Ibid., p. 38.
23 Ibid., p. 43.
24 Ibid., p. 47.
25 Ibid., p. 51. Parry adds that it would be good 'if some small pieces of wood or plaster could fall from the roof onto their heads'.
26 Ibid., p. 52.
27 Ibid., p. 56.
28 Ibid., p. 59.
29 Ibid., p. 61.
30 NLW, GPP 1/2. Parry's underlining.
31 Ibid.
32 Ibid.
33 Parry, introduction to *Tŷ ar y Tywod*, p. 9.
34 Huw Ethall, 'Eisteddfod y Barri a'r Fro', *Y Genhinen* (autumn 1968), 79.
35 See 'Barn myfyrwyr o Goleg y Drindod, Caerfyrddin am *Tŷ ar y Tywod*', *Llwyfan*, 2 (spring 1969), 10.
36 'Radio a theledu', *Baner ac Amserau Cymru* (2 January 1969), 8.

37 'Meic', 'Awr a hanner o ddiflastod gyda'r gwrth-arwr', *Y Cymro* (2 January 1969), 24.
38 'Radio a theledu', ibid.
39 NLW, GPP 1/2.

5

1 National Library of Wales [NLW], Gwenlyn Parry Papers [GPP] 7/1.
2 NLW GPP, 7/3. Notes of funeral oration for Huw Lloyd Edwards. This kind of playful banter was a staple of life in Parry's circle at this time: in NLW, GPP 7/3, there is a copy of a charge sheet made out to Wil Napoleon, accusing him 'between the 4th and 7th day of April, 1972 at Pioneer Chinese Restaurant, 21 Pool Street, Caernarvon, in the Parish of Llanbeblig in the County of Caernarvon' of having 'by a certain deception, namely by falsely implying that you had the means to pay, dishonestly obtained a Curry Beef and one Coffee to the value of 50p. belonging to Stephen Chung, with the intention of permanently depriving the said Stephen Chung of it Contrary to Section 15(1) of the Theft Act, 1968.' There is also a memorable, albeit brief, exchange between Parry and 'Bobi Jones' in 1981, on official notepaper of Yr Academi Gymreig, in NLW, GPP 7/1. There is, of course, no evidence to suggest that such correspondence is genuine, nor that it was ever sent to its intended recipient.
3 Meredydd Evans, interview, 19 October 2011. Joye Evans Parry also recalls seeing Gwenlyn being filmed during a *Cymdeithas* protest against monolingual English road signs in Swansea in 1971.
4 A later affirmation of his political conscience was to join *y Gymdeithas's* campaign for a new Welsh Language Act in 1983 by refusing to pay his bill for water rates because the demand form had been printed in English only. He continued his principled objection even after being assured that he could fill in the monolingual English form in Welsh; and it was only the intercession of Plaid Cymru that persuaded him to pay while they took the Welsh Water Board to the High Court to contest the legality of their actions. NLW, GPP 7/1. Correspondence dated 26 January and 1 February 1983.
5 Rhydderch T. Jones, *Ryan* (Mumbles, Swansea: Black Mountain Press, 1980), p. 102.
6 Ibid., p. 103.
7 NLW, GPP 5/5.
8 Gwenlyn Parry, interviewed on BBC Radio Cymru, *Beti a'i Phobol*: first broadcast 25 February 1988.

[9]   NLW, GPP 5/5.

[10]   NLW, GPP 7/1. Correspondence dated February 1976.

[11]   NLW, GPP 5/5.

[12]   NLW, GPP 5/2. Miscellaneous notes for lecture, undated.

[13]   Joye Evans Parry, interview 6 August 2012.

[14]   Gwenlyn Parry, *Y Ffin* (Llandybïe: Christopher Davies, 1975), p. 18.

[15]   Ibid., p. 25.

[16]   Ibid., pp. 46–7.

[17]   Ibid., p. 65.

[18]   Ibid., pp. 92–3.

[19]   Jan Kott, *Shakespeare our Contemporary* (London: Methuen, 1965), p. 115.

[20]   Parry, *Y Ffin*, p. 19.

[21]   Samuel Beckett, *Endgame* (London: Faber and Faber, 1958), p. 38.

[22]   NLW, GPP 5/5.

[23]   Arthur Morris Jones, 'Dramau'r Eisteddfod II', *Baner ac Amserau Cymru* (31 August 1973), 2.

[24]   Gwilym R. Jones, 'Neges "Y Ffin"?', *Baner ac Amserau Cymru* (19 October 1973), 3.

[25]   Charles Huws, 'Radio a theledu', *Baner ac Amserau Cymru* (21 March 1975), 1.

6

[1]   R. M. Jones, 'Gwenlyn Bunyan', in *Llenyddiaeth Gymraeg 1936–72* (Llandybïe: Christopher Davies, 1975), p. 417.

[2]   'Pobol y BBC', *Y Cymro* (11 August 1966), 12.

[3]   Hefin Wyn, National Library of Wales [NLW], Gwenlyn Parry Papers [GPP] 5/3. Draft notes of an interview with Gwenlyn concerning the 200th episode of *Pobol y Cwm*.

[4]   See Gruffudd Parry, *Cofio'n Ôl* (Caernarfon: Gwasg Gwynedd, 2000), p. 140.

[5]   NLW, GPP 5/2. Lecture notes from 1981. For Fiedler's original quote, see Leslie A. Fiedler, *Love and Death in the American Novel* (New York: Criterion Books, 1960), p. 270.

[6]   Parry, *Cofio'n Ôl*, p. 140.

[7]   See David Jenkins, 'Aber-porth: a study of a coastal village in south Cardiganshire', in Elwyn Davies and Alwyn D. Rees (eds), *Welsh Rural Communities* (Cardiff: University of Wales Press, 1960), pp. 12–23.

[8]   Charles Huws, 'Radio a theledu', *Baner ac Amserau Cymru* (24 January 1975), 1.

⁹ NLW, GPP 2/6. This suggestion is followed by the question '(Can Max act do you think?)'.

¹⁰ Ibid. Parry's underlining.

¹⁰ Gwenlyn Parry, interviewed for *A Welsh Viewpoint*, BBC Wales: first broadcast on 1 March, 1989.

7

1 It is worth noting that Bruce Griffiths intriguingly suggests another possible derivation for the Tower, in the tower block which is the location for Boris Vian's 1959 play *The Empire Builders*. This had been staged in London in 1962. See Bruce Griffiths, 'Dringo dau dŵr: Gwenlyn Parry a Boris Vian', in Bruce Griffiths et al., 'Y Tŵr' *Gwenlyn Parry: Pedair Trafodaeth ar y Ddrama* (Astudiaethau Theatr Cymru, 8; Cricieth: Cymdeithas Theatr Cymru, 1996), pp. 1–6.

2 Gwenlyn Parry, *Y Tŵr* (Llandysul: Gomer, 1979), p. 13.

3 Ibid.

4 National Library of Wales [NLW], Gwenlyn Parry Papers [GPP] 1/5. English synopsis of *Y Tŵr*.

5 Parry, *Y Tŵr*, p. 14.

6 Ibid., p. 17.

7 NLW, GPP 1/5.

8 See Dewi Z. Phillips, 'Bywyd a dieithrio yn *Y Tŵr*', in Dewi Z. Phillips, *Dramâu Gwenlyn Parry* (2nd edn; Caernarfon: Gwasg Pantycelyn, 1995), pp. 91–127.

9 Parry, *Y Tŵr*, p. 19.

10 NLW, GPP 1/5.

11 Parry, *Y Tŵr*, p. 39.

12 Ibid., p. 28.

13 Ibid., p. 38.

14 Ibid., p. 44.

15 NLW, GPP 1/5.

16 Parry, *Y Tŵr*, p. 45.

17 Ibid., pp. 55–6.

18 Ibid., p. 28.

19 See Elan Closs Stephens, 'Gramadeg Gwenlyn', *Barn* (October 2001), 54.

20 Parry, *Y Tŵr*, p. 75.

21 Ibid., p. 76.

22 Ibid., p. 77.

23 Ibid., p. 83. The joke involves a pun on the English 'more' and the Welsh '*môr*', meaning 'sea'. The joke appears as a traditional saying

addressed to English tourists in Caradog Pritchard's unpublished radio draft of *Un Nos Ola Leuad*, p. 80. See NLW, GPP 3/1.

24 Parry, *Y Tŵr*, p. 88.

25 Ibid., p. 101.

26 Ibid., p. 107.

27 Ibid., p. 108.

28 Ibid., p. 109.

29 Saunders Lewis, introduction to Parry, *Y Tŵr*, p. 11.

30 Parry, interviewed for *O Vaughan i Fynwy*, HTV Cymru: first broadcast on S4C, 26 October 1989.

31 Povey's comment on his appointment to the BBC as an assistant script editor in 1973 reveals the extent to which Parry realized that his position at the BBC required him to secure not only his own reputation but also a strong continuity of younger writers thereafter: 'Unofficially, [Gwenlyn] had suggested that I should go for it, but after the interview . . . I wasn't particularly confident, nor did I feel that I had landed the job . . . It seems the rest of the interview panel didn't want to give it to me, but Gwenlyn had sensed an *enaid hoff cytûn* ['kindred spirit'] and pushed things through.' See Meic Povey, *Nesa Peth i Ddim* (Llanrwst: Gwasg Carreg Gwalch, 2010), p. 86.

32 The *Celwrn* was a name given to the 'endlessly flowing pot of wines and gins and beer and whatever else' that was habitually taken of an afternoon. Sion Eirian, interviewed in *Cofio Gwenlyn* (John Hefin (dir.): Cambrensis, 2001).

33 Sion Eirian, interview, 22 October 2011.

8

1 Rhydderch Jones, introduction to Gwenlyn Parry, *Sal* (Llandysul: Gomer, 1982), p. 10.

2 Parry, *Sal*, p. 23.

3 Gwenan Mared Roberts, 'Llwgu a llais y ferch?', *Taliesin* (Eisteddfod 2002), 20.

4 Parry, *Sal*, p. 37.

5 Roberts, 'Llwgu a llais y ferch?', 20.

6 Parry, *Sal*, p. 108: cited in Roberts, 'Llwgu a llais y ferch?', 25–6.

7 Ibid., 22–3.

8 Parry, *Sal*, p. 54.

9 Jean Duvignaud, 'The theatre in society: society in the theatre', in E. Burns and T. Burns (eds), *The Sociology of Literature and Drama* (Harmondsworth: Penguin Education, 1973), p. 89.

¹⁰ Parry, *Sal*, p. 121.

¹¹ Roberts, 'Llwgu a llais y ferch?', 27.

¹² Ibid., 28.

¹³ Eigra Lewis Roberts, 'Digon o ddeunydd i gredinwyr ac anghredinwyr', *Y Cymro* (1 April 1980), 11.

¹⁴ Jones, introduction to *Sal*, p. 9.

9

¹ A copy of the title page of *Y Tŵr* is in Parry's collected papers at the National Library of Wales. A note of dedication in Parry's hand, 'With thanks again for everything, Gwenlyn x', has been supplemented with the words 'and the pain that can never be healed Thanks very much to you', along with the words 'A pity that the tower couldn't come down on you.' The play's note of dedication to Gwenlyn's father has been erased and the words 'Do not talk about him ever again' written alongside. See National Library of Wales [NLW], Gwenlyn Parry Papers [GPP] 1/5.

² Gareth Miles, 'Gwenlyn: y dyn a'r dehongliad', *Sbec* (5–11 March 1988), 10–11. Abel Huws and Mari Lewis are central characters in *Rhys Lewis* (1885), by the great Victorian novelist Daniel Owen.

³ Ibid.

⁴ Rhydderch T. Jones, *Ryan* (Mumbles, Swansea: Black Mountain Press, 1980), p. 130.

⁵ Gwenlyn Parry, *Panto* (Llandysul: Gomer, 1992), p. 23.

⁶ NLW, GPP 5/5.

⁷ Parry, *Panto*, pp. 26–7.

⁸ Ibid., p. 1.

⁹ Ibid., pp. 20–1.

¹⁰ Ibid., p. 51.

¹¹ Ibid., p. 58.

¹² Ibid., p. 64.

¹³ Ibid., p. 65.

¹⁴ In this respect, it is worth noting that in the manuscript version of the play, there is a remark inside the front cover: ' "We are asleep and dreaming and we awake the moment that we die!" Gw.' See NLW, GPP 1/6.

¹⁵ Parry, *Panto*, pp. 4–5. The original Gomer edition has the colloquial 'D'o 'mi sws' for '*Gi' 's a kiss*' rather than the more grammatically correct (but less characterful) 'Dyro i mi sws' found in J. Elwyn Hughes

(ed.), *Dramâu Gwenlyn Parry: Y Casgliad Cyflawn* (Llandysul: Gomer, 2001), p. 334. But the *Casgliad Cyflawn* instantly redeems itself by correcting a misprint in the original which rendered 'Sws!' (*'Kiss!'*) as 'Siws!' (*'Shoes!'*, possibly?). I have combined both versions here.

16 Ibid., p. 56.

17 Ibid., p. 60. The extent to which such fears may have played on Gwenlyn's mind are attested by the fact that, in dedicating *Panto* 'To Ann Beynon, my wife and my love', he added the jocular suffix '– *because I do know!*' See Parry, *Panto*, dedication page.

18 Ibid., p. 64.

19 Sue Roderick, interviewed in *Cofio Gwenlyn* (John Hefin (dir.): Cambrensis, 2001).

20 See NLW, GPP 7/1. Maureen Rhys's congratulatory note to Gwenlyn after the Monday night performance, undated.

21 Eleri Rogers, 'Y gynulleidfa fel clai yn nwylo'r crochenydd', *Y Cymro* (13 August 1986), 7.

10

1 Quoted in Annes Gruffydd's introduction to J. Elwyn Hughes (ed.), *Dramâu Gwenlyn Parry: Y Casgliad Cyflawn* (Llandysul: Gomer, 2001), p. vii.

2 Gwenlyn Parry, *Beti a'i Phobol*, BBC Radio Cymru: first broadcast 25 February 1988.

3 'Gwenlyn Parry', in Eleri Hopcyn (ed.), *Dylanwadau* (Llandysul: Gomer, 1995), p. 55.

4 Gwenlyn Parry, *A Welsh Viewpoint*, BBC Wales: first broadcast 1 March 1989.

5 Sion Eirian, interview, 22 October 2011.

6 Meic Povey, *Nesa Peth i Ddim* (Llanrwst: Gwasg Carreg Gwalch, 2010), p. 189.

7 'Bore Bach', *Taliesin* (March 1992), 10. Parry uses 'Beckett' for 'Becket'.

8 Ann Beynon, interview, 5 November 2011.

9 Harri Pritchard Jones, 'Gwenlyn Parry, 1932–1991', *Taliesin*, 76 (March 1992), 9.

10 Obituary: John Hefin, , 'Gwenlyn Parry', *The Independent* (8 November 1991), 14.

11 Elan Closs Stephens, 'Saer lluniau', *Golwg* (14 November 1991), 9.

12 Povey, *Nesa Peth i Ddim*, pp. 92–3.

13 Jones, 'Gwenlyn Parry, 1932–1991', 9.

14 '[E]in DMG (Dramodydd Mwya'r Genedl/Ganrif/Gymraeg)'. Sian Wyn Siencyn, 'Sbec ar bedwar ec', *Y Faner* (2 October 1987), 21.

Postscript

1 National Library of Wales [NLW], Gwenlyn Parry Papers [GPP] 5/4 contains a number of draft scripts for *Vera Lynn a 'Nhad*, including an extended plot outline; a notebook containing a list of scenes with various ideas for specific shots and lines of dialogue; and a series of index cards listing and describing the main scenes to be included in the screenplay. Where there is a definite correlation between these sources, I have placed occasional details from the notebook and card index into the plot outline. These are marked by square brackets.

Select Bibliography

Material by Gwenlyn Parry

Published plays
Tair Drama Fer (Denbigh: Gwasg Gee, 1965).
Saer Doliau (Llandybïe: Llyfrau'r Dryw, 1966).
Tŷ ar y Tywod (Llandybïe: Christopher Davies, 1969).
Y Ffin (Swansea: Christopher Davies, 1973).
Y Tŵr (Llandysul: Gomer, 1979).
Sal (Llandysul: Gomer, 1982).
Panto (Llandysul: Gomer, 1992).
Dramâu Gwenlyn Parry: Y Casgliad Cyflawn, J. Elwyn Hughes (ed.) (Llandysul: Gomer, 2001).

Selected unpublished works
'Perla' Siwan' (unpublished typescript: National Library of Wales [NLW], Ms Alwen Griffith donation May 2002, ex 2153).
'Vera Lynn a 'Nhad' (unpublished notes: NLW, Gwenlyn Parry Papers (GPP) 5/4.

Other works
'Bore Bach', *Taliesin*, 76 (March 1992), 10.
Grand Slam (John Hefin (dir.): 30th Anniversary edn; Green Umbrella, 2006).

Selected articles
'Rhydd', in Patrick Hannan (ed.), *Wales in Vision: The People and Politics of Television* (Llandysul: Gomer, 1990), pp. 77–84.
'Rhydd', *Taliesin*, 61 (March 1988), 74–9.
'Y busnes sgrifennu 'ma', *Llwyfan*, 2 (spring 1969), 15.

Interviews and biographical material

'Dyddiau Llundain', *Taliesin*, 76 (March 1992), 11–13.

'Gwenlyn Parry', in Eleri Hopcyn (ed.), *Dylanwadau* (Llandysul: Gomer, 1995), pp. 37–56.

'Gwenlyn Parry yn deud ei stori', *Antur*, 15/5 (May 1979), 11, 16.

Interview with Emyr Edwards, 'Dramateiddio ansicrwydd', *Barn* (August/September 1992), 27–9.

Interview with John Stuart Roberts (unpublished incomplete transcript: NLW, GPP 5/5).

Selected radio and television appearances

A Welsh Viewpoint, BBC Wales: first broadcast on 1 March 1989.

Beti a'i Phobol, BBC Radio Cymru: first broadcast 25 February 1988.

Darlithoedd y Pentan: Arf y Diafol neu Arf Duw, Ffilmiau Llifon: first broadcast on S4C, 20 September 1987.

Dawn, HTV Cymru Wales: first broadcast on S4C, 13 December 1983.

Dylanwadau: Gwenlyn Parry, BBC Radio Cymru: series first broadcast 11–15 September 1989.

Gwenlyn, BBC Cymru Wales: first broadcast on S4C, 6 March 1988.

O Vaughan i Fynwy, HTV Cymru Wales: first broadcast on S4C, 26 October 1989.

Material about Gwenlyn Parry

Documentaries

Cofio Gwenlyn (John Hefin (dir.): Cambrensis, 2001).

Selected interviews and biographical material

Beynon, Ann, interviewed for BBC website: *http://www.bbc.co.uk/cymru/gwenlyn/dramodydd/atgofion_ab.shtml*. Accessed 18 November 2012.

Griffith, Llynwen et al., comments submitted to BBC website: *http://www.bbc.co.uk/cymru/gwenlyn/dramodydd/cofioncyhoedd.shtml*. Accessed 18 November 2012.

Jones, William, interviewed for BBC website: *http://www.bbc.co.uk/cymru/gwenlyn/dramodydd/atgofion_wj.shtml*. Accessed 18 November 2012.

'Marged yn dringo'r tŵr', *Atolwg* [supplement in *Golwg*] (8 November 2001), 1.

Miles, Gareth, 'Gwenlyn: y dyn a'r dehongliad', *Sbec* (5–11 March 1988), 10–11.

Ogwen, John, interviewed for BBC website: *http://www.bbc.co.uk/cymru/ gwenlyn/dramodydd/atgofion_jo.shtml.* Accessed 18 November 2012.

Owen, George P., interviewed for BBC website: *http://www.bbc.co.uk/cymru/ gwenlyn/dramodydd/atgofion_geo.shtml.* Accessed 18 November 2012.

Owen, Gwilym, interviewed for BBC website: *http://www.bbc.co.uk/cymru/ gwenlyn/dramodydd/atgofion_gwo.shtml.* Accessed 18 November 2012.

Parry, Joye Evans, interviewed for BBC website: *http://www.bbc.co.uk/ cymru/gwenlyn/dramodydd/atgofion_jp.shtml.* Accessed 18 November 2012.

'Pobol y BBC', *Y Cymro* (11 August 1966), 12.

Rhys, Maureen, interviewed for BBC website: *http://www.bbc.co.uk/cymru/ gwenlyn/dramodydd/atgofion_mr.shtml.* Accessed 18 November 2012.

Roberts, Huw, 'Nes na'r hanesydd?', *Cyntedd* (Fishguard National Eisteddfod edn, 1986), 4.

Tributes

'Cymru'n colli'r saer dramau', *Y Cymro* (13 November 1991), 10.

Evans, Meredydd, 'Gwenlyn Parry (1932–1991)', *Barn* (December 1991), 9–10.

Hefin, John, 'Gwenlyn Parry', *The Independent* (8 November 1991), 14.

Jones, Harri Pritchard, 'A playwright of stature', *New Welsh Review*, 4/3 (winter 1991/92), 62–3.

— 'Gwenlyn Parry, 1932–1991', *Taliesin*, 76 (March 1992), 6–9.

'Nodi degawd ers ymadawiad buan y saer geiriau', *Y Cymro* (3 November 2001), 12.

Ogwen, John, 'Boi bach o Lambabs', *Taliesin*, 76 (March 1992), 17–19.

— *Gwenlyn Parry: Teyrnged*, BBC Radio Cymru: first broadcast 5 November 1991.

Phillips, Dewi Z., 'Gwenlyn Parry (1932–1991)', *Barn* (December 1991), 12–13.

Povey, Meic, 'Os mêts', *Golwg* (14 November 1991), 8.

Rees, D. Ben, 'Gwenlyn Parry 1932–1991', *Planet*, 90 (December 1991/ January 1992), 119–20.

Roberts, Wilbert Lloyd, 'Gwenlyn Parry (1932–1991)', *Barn* (December 1991), 11–12.

Stephens, Elan Closs, 'Saer Lluniau', *Golwg* (14 November 1991), 9.

Y Celfyddydau, BBC Radio Cymru: first broadcast 31 October 2001.

Poems dedicated to Gwenlyn Parry

Edwards, Emyr, 'Gwenlyn: (dramodydd y ddelwedd estynedig)', *Cerddi'r Theatr* ([Llanrwst]: Gwasg Carreg Gwalch, 2008), p. 13.

Williams, Rhydwen, 'Gwenlyn' (unpublished: NLW, GPP 7/4).

Critical works and selected reviews

Baines, Menna, 'Ailddringo'r Tŵr', *Barn* (November 1995), 28–9.

'Barn myfyrwyr o Goleg y Drindod, Caerfyrddin am *Tŷ ar y Tywod'*, *Llwyfan*, 2 (spring 1969), 10.

Clancy, Joseph P., 'Gwenlyn Parry a barddoniaeth theatr', *Ysgrifau Beirniadol*, 21 (1996), 212–21.

— 'Gwenlyn Parry and the poetry of theatre', in *idem, Other Words: Essays on Poetry and Translation* (Cardiff: University of Wales Press, 1999), pp. 110–18.

'Drama gynhyrfus ar daith', *Baner ac Amserau Cymru* (7 April 1966), 1.

Dwyryd, Eleanor, 'Noson gyntaf "Saer Doliau" ', *Baner ac Amserau Cymru* (28 April 1966), 2.

Edwards, Emyr, 'Astudiaeth Dewi Z. Phillips o waith y dramodydd Gwenlyn Parry', *Efrydiau Athronyddol*, 46 (1983), 26–46.

Elis, Meg, 'Arswyd arhosol', *Barn* (December 1995/January 1996), 50.

Griffiths, Bruce et al., *'Y Tŵr' Gwenlyn Parry: Pedair Trafodaeth ar y Ddrama* (Astudiaethau Theatr Cymru, 8; Cricieth: Cymdeithas Theatr Cymru, 1996).

Ifans, Rhiannon, '"O fentro mynd ato, y mae siawns, siawns, iti achub dy hun ac einioes dy genedl": rhai sylwadau ar grefydd yn y ddrama Gymraeg', *Llên Cymru*, 26 (2003), 87–105.

Jones, Arthur Morris, 'Dramau'r Eisteddfod II', *Baner ac Amserau Cymru* (31 August 1973), 2.

Jones, Dafydd Glyn, 'Y ddrama rhyddiaith', in Geraint Bowen (ed.), *Y Traddodiad Rhyddiaith yn yr Ugeinfed Ganrif* (Llandysul: Gomer, 1976), pp. 211–40.

— 'Theatr, drama a llenyddiaeth', *Baner ac Amserau Cymru* (15 August 1968), 8.

Jones, Gwilym R., 'Neges "Y Ffin"?', *Baner ac Amserau Cymru* (19 October 1973), 3.

Jones, Harri Pritchard, 'Saer Doliau', *Baner ac Amserau Cymru* (19 May 1966), 5.

Jones, R. M., 'Gwenlyn Bunyan', in *Llenyddiaeth Gymraeg 1936–72* (Llandybïe: Christopher Davies, 1975), pp. 415–21.

Jones, W. J., 'Gwenlyn Parry – dyn y theatr (1)', *Barn* (April 1996), 37–8.

— 'Gwenlyn Parry – dyn y theatr (2)', *Barn* (May 1996), 38–9.

— 'Gwenlyn Parry – dyn y theatr (3)', *Barn* (June 1996), 51–3.

'Ledled Cymru', *Baner ac Amserau Cymru* (28 April 1966), 4.

Lewis, William R., 'Gwenlyn y dramodydd', *Taliesin*, 76 (March 1992), 14–16.

Owen, Gwilym, 'Clod yn rhy hwyr', *Golwg* (15 November 2001), 26.

Phillips, Dewi Z., 'Byd y Saer Doliau', *Ysgrifau Beirniadol*, IV (March 1969), 306–36.

— *Dramâu Gwenlyn Parry* (2nd edn; Caernarfon: Gwasg Pantycelyn, 1995).

Price, Rhian, 'Gwaith y saer', *Golwg* (25 October 2001), 18–19.

Pritchard, Marged, 'Gwenlyn Parry', in *Portreadau'r Faner*, 3 (Y Bala: Llyfrau'r Faner, 1976), 115–25.

Roberts, Gwenan Mared, 'Gwenlyn', *Barn* (October 2001), 48–53.

— 'Llwgu a llais y ferch?', *Taliesin* (Eisteddfod 2002), 15–29.

— 'O ydio yno?', *Barn* (April 2004), 52–5.

— 'Y ffair a'r tŷ', *Barn* (July/August 2005), 88–90.

Roberts, Eigra Lewis, 'Digon o ddeunydd i gredinwyr ac anghredinwyr', *Y Cymro* (1 April 1980), 11.

Roberts, John, 'Gwenlyn, Pozzo a Lucky', *Esgyrn* (summer 1978) [typescript available in NLW, GPP 5/3].

Rogers, Eleri, 'Y gynulleidfa fel clai yn nwylo'r crochenydd', *Y Cymro* (13 August 1986), 7.

Rowlands, John, 'Saer Doliau a'r theatr ddwl', *Y Traethodydd* (October 1968), 157–67.

Stephens, Elan Closs, 'Gramadeg Gwenlyn', *Barn* (October 2001), 54–5.

— 'Gwenlyn Parry', *Taliesin*, 63 (July 1988), 51–9.

— *Y Moderneiddwyr* (Caernarfon: Gwynedd County Council, 2001).

— 'Panto', *Barn* (September 1995), 50–1.

— 'Panto', *Barn* (October 1995), 36–7.

— 'Panto', *Barn* (November 1995), 53–5.

— 'Panto', *Barn* (December 1995/January 1996), 83–5.

— 'Panto', *Barn* (March 1996), 60–2.

— 'Y Twr', *Barn* (March 1995), 50–2.

— 'Y Twr (ii)', *Barn* (April 1995), 38–40.

— 'Y Twr (iii)', *Barn* (May 1995), 39–41.

— 'Y Twr (iv)', *Barn* (June 1995), 47–50.

Tomos, Nia Wynn, 'Cyfeiriadau newydd yn y ddrama Gymraeg *c*.1950–1980, gyda sylw arbennig i weithiau Huw Loyd Edwards, W. S. Jones a Gwenlyn Parry' (unpublished MA thesis, University of Wales, Aberystwyth, 1983).

Tudur, Non, 'Panto ydy bywyd', *Golwg* (26 February 2004), 22–3.

Williams, J. S., 'Saer Doliau (Gwenlyn Parry)', *Baner ac Amserau Cymru* (6 October 1966), 4.

Other works cited

'Aprad', 'Saer Cyboliau', *Barn* (November 1966), 13.

Duvignaud, Jean, 'The theatre in society: society in the theatre', in E. Burns and T. Burns (eds), *The Sociology of Literature and Drama* (Harmondsworth: Penguin Education, 1973).

Gwynfryn, Hywel, *Hugh Griffith* (Llandysul: Gomer, 2010).

Hefin, John (ed.), *Grand Slam: Behind the Scenes of the Classic Film* (Talybont: Y Lolfa, 2007).

Jones, Dafydd Glyn, 'Peth o'r gwir am lwyth o gelwydd', *Barn* (March 2009), 47–51.

Jones, J. R., *Yr Argyfwng Gwacter Ystyr* (Llandybïe: Llyfrau'r Dryw, 1964).

Jones, Rhydderch T., *Ryan* (Mumbles, Swansea: Black Mountain Press, 1980).

Kott, Jan, *Shakespeare our Contemporary* (London: Methuen, 1965).

Lewis, William R., 'Huw Lloyd Edwards: comedïwr, moesolwr a bardd', *Taliesin*, 61 (March 1988), 46–58.

Morgan, Sharon, *Hanes Rhyw Gymraes* (Talybont: Y Lolfa, 2011).

Parry, Gruffudd, *Cofio'n Ôl* (Caernarfon: Gwasg Gwynedd, 2000).

Parry, Rhiannon, 'O lygad y ffynnon', *Barn* (March 2009), 51–4.

Povey, Meic, *Nesa Peth i Ddim* (Llanrwst: Gwasg Carreg Gwalch, 2010).

Robinson, John A. T., *Honest to God* (London: SCM Press, 1963).

'Taliesin' [D. Tecwyn Lloyd], ' "Y Ffynnon" a chyflwyniad', *Taliesin*, 56 (July 1986), 38–48.

Williams, John Roberts, 'Mons', *Taliesin*, 61 (March 1988), 44.

Žižek, Slavoj, *The Pervert's Guide to the Cinema* (Sophie Fiennes (dir.): Amoeba Film, 2006).

Adjudications

Davies, Eic, 'Drama fer wreiddiol', in J. T. Jones (ed.), *Cyfansoddiadau a Beirniadaethau Eisteddfod Genedlaethol Frenhinol Cymru Dyffryn Maelor 1961* (Llandysul: Gomer on behalf of the Court of the National Eisteddfod, 1961), pp. 158–61.

Davies, W., 'Drama fer i blant ysgolion uwchradd', in *Cyfansoddiadau a Beirniadaethau Eisteddfod Genedlaethol Genedlaethol Frenhinol Cymru Abertawe a'r Cylch 1964* (Llandysul: Gomer on behalf of the Court of the National Eisteddfod, 1964), pp. 201–3.

Humphreys, Emyr, 'Drama wreiddiol fer', in Stephen J. Williams (ed.), *Cyfansoddiadau a Beirniadaethau Eisteddfod Genedlaethol Frenhinol Cymru Llanelli a'r Cylch 1962* (Llandysul: Gomer on behalf of the Court of the National Eisteddfod, 1962), pp. 211–13.

Williams, J. Ellis, 'Drama wreiddiol fer', in William Morris (ed.), *Cyfansoddiadau a Beirniadaethau Eisteddfod Genedlaethol Frenhinol Cymru Llandudno a'r Cylch 1963* (Llandysul: Gomer on behalf of the Court of the National Eisteddfod, 1963), pp. 172–4.

INDEX